The Genesis Solution

The Genesis Solution

Kenneth A. Ham

and

Paul S. Taylor

BAKER BOOK HOUSE
Grand Rapids, Michigan 49516

Contents

Acknowledgments

Several years ago, as I was helping to establish the Creation ministry in Australia, I first saw a motion picture called *The World That Perished,* produced by Films For Christ. It provided dramatic support for the Genesis Flood, including exciting evidence that any layman could understand. I was extremely impressed with both the professionalism and the content of the film and started using it extensively throughout Australia. The response was tremendous, in churches and public schools alike. For the first time, thousands were dramatically presented with the truth concerning Creation, Noah's Flood, and the warning of coming judgment. As a result, many were moved to accept Christ as their Savior.

Thus I first became acquainted with the powerful ministry of Films For Christ, headquartered in Mesa, Arizona. This organization is a non-profit mission committed to producing films that proclaim to the world the truth about Creation. Their motion pictures are widely translated and reach millions in over forty-five nations. I went on to use other Films For Christ productions to great effect *(ORIGINS: How the World Came to Be* and *The Great Dinosaur Mystery)*. All played an important part in the growth of our Creation ministry in Australia and helped educate great numbers of people.

I would like to sincerely thank Films For Christ, and in particular Marian and Paul Taylor and Dale Mason, for their support of my ministry and their commitment to Creationism as a whole. They wholeheartedly share my urgent burden to teach Christians about the foundational importance of the Creation message. Their production of *The Genesis Solution* (film, video, and book) makes a substantial contribution to the ministry of educating the Christian public on these vital matters.

Ken Ham

1

Two Religions in Conflict

What Should Christians Think About Genesis?

Many Christians are confused about the Book of Genesis, wondering how it should be interpreted. No portion is more hotly debated than the first eleven chapters, which describe Creation, the Fall, the Flood, and the Tower of Babel miracle. Some say these chapters should be interpreted as allegories or poetic story lessons, while others claim they are merely adaptations of ancient, pagan legends taken from the Babylonians and Sumerians. Other Christians, not willing to write off these chapters completely, suggest that some parts are factual, while others should not be taken literally. Still others, including those in the modern-day Creation Science movement, believe that Genesis should be understood quite literally as a highly accurate record of important historical events.

How important is the Genesis account to Christianity? What should the Christian position be toward Evolution, the internationally popular belief that says matter and life itself started billions of years ago and changed upwardly into their present states via natural processes? As long as Christians believe in God, does it make any real difference whether they believe he created the world "instantaneously" in six literal days—or slowly over billions of years?

Is Evolution an Unimportant Side Issue?

Many Christians believe that the Creation/Evolution debate is a side issue and thus not relevant to everyday Christian life. For example, someone might say with a bit of sarcasm, "After all, who's really interested in rubidium-strontium dating, ontogeny, and phylogeny and all that other obscure, technical jargon? We have plenty of important issues to worry about, like abortion, pornography, homosexuality, and AIDS."

Unfortunately, most Christians have misunderstood what the Creation/Evolution battle is really all about, which may be why millions of modern people have lined up in partial or wholehearted support of various practices and beliefs that are in opposition to Christian values and beliefs. Cultural acceptance of homosexuality, abortion, premarital and extramarital sex, easy divorce, pornography, agnosticism, atheism, Secular Humanism, and the removal of God from public education and civic events have support from large numbers of people. To truly understand why, we must search for any common foundation that these issues may share. As we shall see, that foundation is the evolutionary theory, which is accepted as fact by millions, as are its many ramifications. *Evolution has seemingly given society a "scientific" justification for rejecting God and his authority as Creator.*

Is This an Issue of Science Versus Religion?

Before we delve into the fascinating connections between the Genesis account and the issues of our day, it is important to understand the true nature of the Creation/Evolution debate. The media have led many to believe this is a battle between "religion" and "science." This is one of the most widely believed misconceptions of our day! Please note these three simple points:

1. *Science cannot directly deal with the past.* Anyone who truly understands what science is about knows that it has

to do with what we can deal with in the *present*—what we can observe and can repeatedly test. The rocks, fossils, and all other forms of physical evidence that scientists are now studying exist in the present, not the past. Scientists cannot go back in time to directly examine the animals and rocks of long ago. They cannot personally observe the past or test it. Scientists are limited to testing and observing things as they exist *now*—in the present.

2. *Evolution is a belief.* Evolutionary theory is a series of beliefs about the past that evolutionists use to try to explain facts that are observable in the present. Evolution is not "science," because science can deal directly only with what is observed in the present. No scientist can go back in time to witness or examine the ancient world of dinosaurs and the early days of mankind. Both Creation *and* Evolution provide ways for explaining the past that are beyond direct scientific examination and verification. Ultimately, both Creation and Evolution are beliefs.

3. *Evolution is a religious belief.* Despite growing scientific evidence against evolutionary theory, many continue to believe in it with great fervency and faith. Since "religion" can be defined as a concept or system of belief that is held to with ardor and faith, ultimately both Creationism and Evolutionism are religious views concerning life. *Therefore, the conflict is really a battle between two religious beliefs.* When governments tell Christians that they cannot provide evidence for Creationism in school "because it is religion"—but they can teach "science"—what are they really saying? "We can't allow Christianity [Creation] to be taught in public schools; we've replaced it with another religion—Secular Humanism [Evolution]."

Scientists—Human or Super-Human?

Many laypeople have an inaccurate view of scientists. Are scientists some unique class of human—super-smart, totally objective, and always seeking the truth, no matter where it might lead?

What are *real* scientists like? Well, they come in only two basic forms: male and female. Scientists are just like everyone else—human, fallible, and biased. And it is important to remember that the beliefs and biases of all people, including scientists, affect their theories, their decisions, their research, and their interpretation of evidence.

There are four common misconceptions about scientists:
Scientists are objective.
Scientists are unbiased.
Science is infallible. If a scientist says it, you can trust it.
A real scientist always wears a white lab coat.

Biases—We All Have Them

The Bias of Atheists

Atheists emphatically believe that "there is no God." But, with that as their bias, whenever they look at evidence, they can never truly allow questions like "Did God create?"

The truth is: scientists are human and, therefore, biased—just like all other human beings. Their theories, research, and interpretation of evidence are affected by their chosen beliefs about life and origins.

or "Could the Bible be true?" or "Could Noah's Flood have happened?" If they even allowed those as options, they would no longer be true atheists.

Even if an atheistic scientist found a big boat (Noah's ark) on the top of Mount Ararat, he might deny that it was proof of the biblical Flood. He would have to claim that it was a religious hoax, coincidence, or something else. Whatever his explanation, he could never accept the Flood judgment as fact and still maintain his atheism.

You see, an atheist is 100-percent biased. Atheists rule out God, including all evidence of his Creation, his miracles, and his judgments on mankind's sin.

The Bias of Agnostics

Agnostics strongly doubt that God exists, although they are not certain enough (or presumptuous enough) to take the more definite position of an atheist. Although they generally believe that "no one can ever truly know *whether* God exists," in practice agnostics live under the assumption that there is no God.

Yet, many agnostics claim, "Look, we're open-minded. We're just sitting here on the fence waiting for you to prove to us that God exists. You bring the proof, and then we'll listen." But what happens when they are presented with such evidence from scientific journals, books, and museums? Almost invariably, that open-minded attitude disappears. Agnostics cannot accept as evidence anything that brings their belief into serious question. Agnostic scientists, too, are biased in what evidence they accept and how they interpret it.

The Bias of Bible-Believing Christians

Christians choose to believe in the existence of God. And, although there is plenty of good evidence to support this belief, it is ultimately a decision of faith. We (the authors) believe that the Bible is accurate and truly God's Word. We believe the Bible gives an authentic, although not exhaustive, history of our planet. Knowing how much evidence has already been found in support of the Bible, we have faith that all our questions will eventually be answered. Therefore, having that bias (belief), we do not accept as final any *interpretation* of evidence that seems to prove there is no God or that clearly contradicts the Bible.

2

Choosing Your Bias

Think about the problem we humans have with "knowledge," whether schoolchildren or Ph.Ds. No human being knows everything. The only way we can be unfailingly certain of coming to the right conclusion about what happened in the ancient past or about almost anything else is if we can be sure that we have total knowledge about it. But we human beings are very finite creatures—so much so that no matter how much any person knows, there is infinitely more to learn. This means that no matter how much we know, we are still infinitely ignorant. Compared to God, we really don't know much at all!

Finite knowledge is a serious problem. This is why man's theories about the past so frequently change. As new evidence is found, theories are modified or abandoned to cope with new data and new methods of interpretation.

Ken participated in a radio debate in which a scientist mentioned the fact that various scientific theories are currently changing. Ken agreed and asked, "Don't they change because man finds knowledge he didn't have before?"

"That's true," said the scientist.

"Well, theories will keep on changing, won't they?" asked Ken.

"Certainly!" he replied.

17

"Isn't that because we don't know everything there is to know about everything?"

"That's right," agreed the scientist.

"In fact, we *never* will know everything, will we?" Ken asked.

"That's true," nodded the scientist.

"That means you can't be sure about Evolution either, can you?" asked Ken.

"Oh, no!" the scientist exclaimed. "Evolution is a fact!"

Once again, we see evidence that Evolution is a belief, not science. Evolution is that scientist's bias and his faith.

Which Bias Is the Best?

In reality, the issue is not whether or not you are biased, but which bias is the best. Which belief system makes the most sense?

Creationism

As relatively ignorant and limited beings, we have no assurance of ever coming to the right conclusions about origins if we start only with human wisdom. In this confusing world, the joyous knowledge for Christians is that the Bible is the Word of the Creator who was there from the very beginning. He is the only truly reliable witness of the past, and he has all the knowledge and wisdom of infinity. This Creator has provided a written record so that we can know what really happened.

Scientists who accept the biblical record can research the evidence of the present (Scientific Creationism) and see if it fits with what has been revealed about the past (Biblical Creationism). And it does! Overwhelmingly so! Never in history has man accumulated more scientific evidence in support of Creationism and against Evolutionism.

Evolutionary theory is a series of beliefs about the *past* that Evolutionists use to try to explain facts that are observable in the *present.* Evolution is not "science," because science can deal only with what is observed in the present.

Despite growing scientific evidence against evolutionary theory, many people continue to believe in it with great fervency and faith. Since "religion" can be defined as a concept or system of belief that is held to with ardor and faith, ultimately both Creationism and Evolutionism are religious views concerning life.

The conflict is really a battle between two religious beliefs:
(1) Belief in divine creation, including the existence of an original paradise and the
    biblical record of man's history and purpose.

(2) Belief in Evolution, with time and chance producing the universe and its organisms.

Atheistic Evolutionism

Due to their bias, scientists who are atheistic evolutionists are limited to theorizing a history based only on observable natural processes. They cannot consider supernatural, outside forces. Evolutionism is a religion without revelation. Atheistic evolutionists do not accept the Bible as a written record from the past, provided by an expert eyewitness who can tell them what really happened.

We Prefer Belief in Creation

In reality, the controversy between Scientific Creationism and Evolutionism is not religion versus science. It is really the science of one religion versus the science of another religion. Christians have good reason to prefer belief in Creation:

1. It fits better with the facts.
2. It has a clear and inherent advantage over Evolutionism, since it is based upon records from someone who was there from the very beginning: the all-knowing Creator.
3. Christians can know the Creator personally.

3

Genesis—
The Foundation of
Christianity

Why are many Christians so vitally concerned about the spread of belief in Evolutionism? It is because evolutionary theory is a direct attack on the Book of Genesis. And Genesis is foundational to Christianity.

There are two passages that underline the New Testament's position on the crucial nature of the writings of Moses, which begin with Genesis:

1. *John 5:45–47.* Jesus Christ said, "But do not think I will accuse you before the Father. Your accuser is Moses. . . . If you believed Moses, you would believe me, for he wrote about me. But since you do not believe what he wrote, how are you going to believe what I say?" Here the very Creator of the world is asking, "If you don't believe the writings of Moses, how in the world are you ever going to believe what I'm saying?"

2. *Luke 16:29–31.* A statement in Luke's Gospel says practically the same thing. In one of Jesus' parables, Lazarus (a beggar) died and went to be with Abraham. The rich man at whose gate the beggar lay died also, but he went to a place of torment. The rich man begged Abraham to allow him to go back so he could warn his brothers about this horrible place of punishment. But he was not allowed to return. So he asked if Lazarus could go back and warn them. We are told that "Abraham replied, 'They have Moses

23

Genesis is foundational to Christianity. Christ quoted from it; the rest of the Bible refers to it or quotes from it more than any other book. If you do not have a believing knowledge of the Book of Genesis, you cannot hope to attain a full comprehension of what Christianity is all about.

and the Prophets; let them listen to them.' 'No, father Abraham,' he [the rich man] said, 'but if someone from the dead goes to them, they will repent.' He said to him, 'If they do not listen to Moses and the Prophets, they will not be convinced even if someone rises from the dead.'"

Throughout both the Old and New Testaments, there are many references to the writings of Moses. In fact, there are more references to one particular book written by Moses than there are to any other. That book is Genesis. In fact, it is the most quoted-from or referred-to book in the entire

Bible. Both Jesus and Paul quoted from it, and Christian doctrine was built upon its foundation. Yet, paradoxically, in many Christian and non-Christian circles alike, Genesis has become the most scoffed at, mocked at, disregarded, allegorized, and mythologized book of all the Holy Scriptures!

Why Is Genesis So Attacked?

Why has the Bible's most respected book become the most attacked in our modern world? Why do the enemies of Christianity put so much effort into defeating that particular book above all others? Because Genesis is the most foundational book of the Bible. And, as the psalmist said, "When the foundations are being destroyed, what can the righteous do?" (Ps. 11:3).

To see the truth of that statement, think about building a house. A building is constructed from the foundations up, for a very important reason. The foundation is crucial to the whole structure. If the foundation is suddenly removed, the structure will almost surely collapse.

In a similar way, Genesis is a foundation for the rest of the Bible. Ultimately, all biblical doctrines of theology (the structure) are based directly or indirectly on the Book of Genesis (the foundation).

The Meaning of Anything Is Connected to Its Origin

To grasp a better understanding of this, think about any one of a number of Christian doctrines. And then think about its origin. The meaning of anything is permanently tied to its origin. For instance, the basic meaning of marriage is connected with its origin, which is found in Genesis 2:7, 18–25—the account of Adam and Eve. The meaning of sin is tied to its origin, which is found in Genesis one through three—the Fall of man from holy perfection to rebellion and evil. The meaning of death is inseparable

from its origin, which is in Genesis 2:16–17; 3:1–6, 19 (cf. Rom. 5:12)—the promised result of sin. The meaning of the seven-day week and the Sabbath is connected with its origin, which goes back to Genesis 2:2 (cf. Exod. 20:8–11). The very message of the gospel has its foundations in Genesis: the entrance of sin, the need for a way of salvation, and the

Would anyone be so foolish as to try to build a house from the roof down, rather than from the foundation up? Of course not! The building must start at the foundation which is so crucial to the whole structure.

prophecy (Gen. 3:15) concerning the One to come who would defeat the serpent. While in Rome, Paul used the writings of Moses, which he accepted as literal, to help explain Jesus and the gospel (Acts 28:23).

These same foundational connections to Genesis are true for all Christian doctrines, either directly or by implication.

All biblical doctrines are based directly or indirectly on the Book of Genesis. All important Christian beliefs are linked in one way or another to Genesis. Is it any wonder this foundational book is the focus of vigorous attacks from the enemies of the gospel?

As Bible scholar and scientist Dr. Henry M. Morris has said, "If the Bible were somehow expurgated of the Book of Genesis, the rest of the Bible would be incomprehensible. It would be like a building without a ground floor, or a bridge with no support."

Is it any wonder that Satan is concentrating his attack on Genesis more than any other book? Evolutionism, in the guise of science, is being used to say, "You can't trust Genesis or the rest of the Bible. Evolution has proven it wrong."

The Foundational Truths of Genesis

Genesis is the original source for many important Christian beliefs and the basis for much Christian doctrine:

1. God was "in the beginning," and he is eternal (Gen. 1:1; 21:33).
2. God is the Creator of the universe and heavens—everything (Gen. 1).
3. Creation is not ongoing; God completed it (Gen. 2:1–2).
4. God created both male and female (Gen. 1:27; 5:2).
5. All human beings are descendants of Adam and Eve (Gen. 1:28a; 3:20).
6. Man is not an animal; he was set above the animals (Gen. 1:26–28; 2:19).
7. We are made in the "image of God" (Gen. 1:27; 5:1), and we have a soul (Gen. 2:7).
8. There is good, and there is evil (Gen. 2:16–17, 3:5, 22; etc.).
9. God is holy and righteous.
10. The original world was a paradise; all was "very good" (Gen. 1:31).
11. Humans were originally sinless.
12. Humans originally walked with God (Gen. 3:8) and had a much closer and more direct relationship with the Creator.
13. God works in human affairs and has done so from the beginning.
14. God sets laws that we are to obey (e.g., Gen. 26:5).
15. God sees all of our sins and has done so from the beginning (Gen. 3:11; 4:10; 6:5; etc.).
16. The circumstances of the first sinful act of man (the test and temptation of "the tree of the knowledge of good and evil").
17. The sin of our original parents, Adam and Eve, is the

reason why all humans are born sinful: the sin
nature is passed from generation to generation.
18. Sin separated man from God (Gen. 3:24).
19. God punishes sin (Gen. 3:14–19; 4:11–12; 6:5–7;
    etc.).
20. Man's sin and God's curse began the corruption and
    decay of paradise (Gen. 3:17, 22–23). The Fall and
    God's curse are ultimate reasons why our world to-
    day is imperfect—filled with problems, suffering and
    evils, both physical and moral.
21. Death came through sin (Gen. 3:19).
22. The origin of God's plan to save man.
23. Woman is *of* the man (Gen. 2:22–23).
24. Woman is *for* the man (Gen. 2:18).
25. "Leave father and mother . . ." (Gen. 2:24).
26. United husband and wife "become one flesh" (Gen.
    2:24).
27. Male headship in the normal marriage relationship
    (Gen. 3:16).
28. Sinfulness of homosexuality and other sexual perver-
    sions (e.g., Gen. 18:20; 19:4–6, 13).
29. Origin of "the chosen people"—Abraham and his de-
    scendants (Gen. 12:1, etc.)
30. And so on. . . .

Five Monumental Happenings in Genesis

There are only five historical events that can truly be
noted as being so important that their effects and ramifications have affected (and continue to affect) *every* human
being on this planet. The first four of these greatest historical events are recorded in Genesis, and the fifth is undeniably connected to all of them:

1. *The Creation* by God of the original world—a paradise.
2. *The Fall of man to sin and the loss of paradise.* This

involved the curse and the origin of "death," God's first great and universal judgment on man's sin.

3. *The Flood*—(God's second great judgment on man's sin—destroyed the entire population of the planet, except for Noah and seven of his family members, and resulted in tremendous environmental, geological, and geographical changes that affect every person to this day.

4. *The Tower of Babel incident* (Gen. 11)—God's third great judgment—is responsible for the multitude of languages that divide mankind to this day.

5. *The Creator born as a man*—Christ's birth, life, death, and resurrection.

Secular evolutionists vigorously deny the occurrence of each of these most important events of history. The result is that much of the world's population is totally ignorant of these five events. Sadly, even most Christians have difficulty naming them!

Genesis is tremendously important to Christianity. *If you do not have a believing knowledge of the Book of Genesis, you cannot hope to attain a full comprehension of what Christianity is all about.* And, of course, you must do more than just believe Genesis is true; you must also understand what it says.

4

The Gospel's Genesis Connection

The wonderful Good News to mankind about Jesus Christ, our Redeemer and Savior, is inseparably connected to the Book of Genesis. Without Genesis, the gospel story is incomplete. If we were totally ignorant of the contents of Genesis, the story of Christ's birth, death, and resurrection would make no real sense.

In brief, what does Genesis reveal? God created Adam and Eve. They were the first human beings and the original parents of every man and woman who has ever been born on this earth. They were pure and without sin and had a special, close relationship with the Creator. God gave them a choice, but they rebelled against God by deciding to reject God's rules and willfully trust their own opinions. This rebellion is called sin. The Bible tells us that—as a result of that sin—God placed the curse of death on the world. All people die because of that original sin. These events are the foundational reason why Jesus came to be crucified on our behalf and raised from the dead. The apostle Paul understood this Genesis link, as can be seen in 1 Corinthians 15, referred to by some as "the definition passage" of the gospel message.

Without Genesis, the gospel story would be incomplete. Genesis is the source document for establishing us as created beings responsible to our Creator. It also reveals that our original parents were pure and without sin, and thus enjoyed a special, very close relationship with the Creator. Genesis provides a brief but tantalizing description of the wondrous paradise our Creator lovingly designed. It was far unlike the pain-filled, sin-worn world of degeneration that we experience today.

Death: Genesis and the Gospel

Some Christians have missed the important fact that both spiritual *and* physical death have their origin in the fall of man to sin. Yet, death's Genesis connection is confirmed by Scripture:

1. "For since death came through a man [the first Adam], the resurrection of the dead comes also through a man [the second Adam]. For as in Adam all die, so in Christ all will be made alive" (1 Cor. 15:21–22). Here Paul is discussing the physical resurrection of Christ and the physical resurrection of believers.
2. "Therefore, just as sin entered the world through one

Our original parents rebelled against God by deciding to reject God's rules and willfully trust their own opinions. This sin severed their close relationship with the Creator.

man [Adam], and death through sin, and in this way death came to all men, because all sinned. . . . death reigned from the time of Adam . . . many died by the trespass of the one man. . . ." (Rom. 5:12, 14–15).

3. God expelled Adam and Eve from the Garden of Eden and guarded the tree of life so they would not use it to thwart death and physically live forever (Gen. 3:22–23).

4. In Old Testament times, God's requirement for the forgiveness of sins was demonstrated through the physical death of sacrificial animals: ". . . without the shedding of blood there is no forgiveness" (Heb. 9:22). Physical death is the clear penalty for sin—first demonstrated by the death of Adam and the sacrificial animals (beginning with those killed by God to clothe Adam and Eve), and ultimately by the death of Christ, the perfect sacrifice and atonement.

5. The Bible clearly teaches that physical death for all living creatures did not exist prior to man's sin. Since the Fall, "We know that the whole creation has been groaning as in the pains of childbirth right up to the present time" (Rom. 8:22). God had originally created a paradise for Adam, free of death and suffering.

No Meat-Eating in the Garden of Eden

The first land-dwelling animals and the birds were created as vegetarians and given the plants as their only source of food (Gen. 1:29–30). Man was also created to be vegetarian (Gen. 1:29) and was not given permission to eat meat until after the Flood (Gen. 9:3). If you wonder about animals like lions that today have sharp teeth and short digestive tracts that work well for meat-eating, here are several things to consider:

1. *All the original land-dwelling animals were vegetarians, including lions.* But God will one day make the lion a vegetarian again (Isa. 11:7).

2. *All animals have degenerated from their original excellence in one degree or another.* The original animals were perfect, but nothing in our fallen world is perfect today. Animals have therefore degenerated—through post-Fall and post-Flood environmental pressures, natural selection, degenerative mutations, and possibly through direct changes by God at the time of the curse. We can only guess at many of the differences between animals of today and those of the original Creation.

3. *Sharp teeth are not a reliable distinguishing feature of carnivores.* Various animals today have sharp teeth and claws but eat only plants (e.g., the panda and the Australian fruit bat). Grizzly bears eat grass and other plant materials almost exclusively (about 90 percent of their diet, some say), and fish and other creatures make up only a small part of their current diet. Sharp teeth are not just good for meat; they are superb tools for cutting and ripping

The final effect of man's rebellion might have been eternal separation from God—forever forfeiting a close and special relationship with the Creator. Holy and righteous, God cannot dwell with sin, nor can he overlook it.

plants and fruits. Today, despite their degeneration from original perfection, most carnivores can still survive quite well on a properly balanced diet of vegetable matter.

Why Did God Send Death into the World?

Many people are frightened of death. Most non-Christians look at the suffering and death in our world and conclude that God must not really be good or loving or even all-powerful. But, surprisingly, the very reason for death is that God *is* a God of love. In fact, Christians should praise God for death!

The final effect of Adam's rebellion might have been eternal separation from God—forever forfeiting man's close and special relationship with the Creator. Holy and absolutely righteous, God cannot dwell with sin, nor can he overlook it. But, because of his love, God set into motion a plan by

Death and degeneration entered the world as a result of man's sin. But the Creator used death to set into motion a marvelous plan to reunite man with him forever. The Creator came to earth in the form of Jesus Christ, died for our sins, and

demonstrated the ultimate power to conquer death. He promised that Creation will be restored to the wondrous excellence he originally designed for us—and death will be no more!

which man could one day be reunited with him forever.
God placed upon man the curse of death: the just penalty
for sin. God then sent his only Son, the Lord Jesus Christ,
to become a man like us and to bring us back to himself.
The perfect, sinless Creator of the universe suffered that
same penalty of death in his own body. He tasted death for
everyone (Heb. 2:9).

Then, demonstrating his righteousness and power, Jesus
rose from the dead. One day he will reign and "put all his
enemies under his feet. The last enemy to be destroyed is
death" (1 Cor. 15:25–26). All who accept Christ as Lord and
Savior will be redeemed and received back by God—ultimately with new and perfect bodies—and spend eternity
with him.

Thus we see that death is the means by which we are
being restored to God and beautiful, holy perfection. *That is
the message of Christianity.* What a wonderful and forgiving
thing God has done and is still doing!

Evolutionism, on the other hand, teaches that death and
bloodshed existed long before man's existence. Thus, this
doctrine attacks the very message of Christianity. (This will
be discussed in more detail in later chapters.)

Paradise Will Be Restored!

For Christians, there is wonderful hope for the future, an
essential part of the ultimate promise of the gospel. One day
God is going "to restore everything, as he promised long ago
through his holy prophets" (Acts 3:21). Yes, the blessed
promise of God is that one day there will be a restoration of
all things to the wondrous excellence that he originally
created!

The description of this restoration, like the description of
the original world, includes no death and no suffering. The
animals will again be vegetarian and at peace with one
another:

"The wolf will live with the lamb, the leopard will lie down with the goat, the calf and the lion and the yearling together; and a little child will lead them. The cow will feed with the bear . . . the lion will eat straw like the ox. . . . They will neither harm nor destroy . . ." (Isa. 11:6–7, 9).

"[God] will swallow up death forever. The Sovereign LORD will wipe away the tears from all faces . . ." (Isa. 25:8).

"He will wipe away every tear from their eyes. There will be no more death or mourning or crying or pain . . ." (Rev. 21:4).

The world will once again be paradise.

Teaching the *Whole* Gospel

Anyone who claims to be teaching the Good News and does not include *all* of its elements is not teaching the whole gospel. The gospel message begins in Genesis and is not complete without the following three basic elements:

1. *The Foundation.* The Creator is all-powerful and all-knowing. God created the universe and all creatures in great excellence. The original world was a paradise where man was in personal contact with the Creator, that pure and righteous God. Today we are abnormal people living in an abnormal world. We fell from paradise when the first man (Adam) rebelled and came under physical and spiritual death—separation from close communion with God. God promised to supply a perfect way of salvation.

2. *The Power.* The all-loving Creator voluntarily came to earth in the person of Jesus Christ as the second Adam and willingly died for Adam's sins and ours. This loving sacrifice paid the necessary price to redeem fallen humanity, providing a way to return us to close communion with God.

Christ rose from the dead, showing that he indeed has the power to defeat death. The Word of God was provided to clearly and reliably reveal this whole story of our origins, our destiny, the way of salvation, and the right way we should live.

3. *The Hope.* Ultimately, Christ will defeat death for all of us (physical and spiritual) and will wipe away all tears and pain (Isa. 7:17; Rev. 21:4). He will set everything right. Paradise will be restored. Man will have an eternal close relationship with our holy and loving Creator.

5

Rejecting the Creator's Authority

Evolutionism is basically atheistic and rejects the Creator's authority. To understand why, we must look at the basic difference between believing in Evolution and believing in the biblically documented Creation.

"Why Can't I Write My Own Rules?"

Consider the following situation. A student who was an evolutionist came to Ken and asked, "Why can't I write my own rules about life and decide what I want to do?"

"You want to write your own rules about life?" Ken questioned.

"Yes, sir."

Ken said, "You can do that if you like, but in that case, why can't I shoot you?"

"You can't do that!" the student responded with surprise.

"Why not?"

"It's not right."

"Why isn't it right?" asked Ken.

"Well, because it's wrong."

"*Why* is it wrong?" Ken probed.

"Well, it's just not right," the student replied in frustration.

"Well, you've got a problem, haven't you?" said Ken. "If

you want to write *your* own rules about life, then how about *me*? Can I write my own rules?"

"Sure, that's only fair."

"Okay, then here is one of my first rules: 'Types like you are dangerous.' If I can find enough people to agree with me, we are going to eliminate you from society." You can guess what the student thought about that!

The student was trapped by the ultimate ramifications of his philosophy. His problem began when he rejected the Creation account. He thus concluded, "Nobody made me. I'm just a product of time and chance. I own myself. I'm my own boss and will write my own rules—and so can everyone else." But he—like most such thinkers—is not ready to endorse that last part entirely.

Only the Creator has the ultimate right to set absolutes:

1. The Creator made us.
2. Therefore, the Creator owns us and everything else in his Creation.
3. As the owner, he has a right to set standards of what is right and what is wrong. He is the absolute authority.
4. What better ruler could we ask for than the One who is all-good, all-powerful, and all-knowing? Who would know better what the rules should be? Only he has the knowledge, wisdom, and right to set absolute standards.

Total Acceptance of Evolutionism Can Lead to Anarchy

If you believe you are simply a product of chance and random evolutionary processes, who owns you? *You* do. Who has a right to make the rules and to decide what is right and wrong? *You* do. But since everyone else also has that same right, the ultimate result will be either chaos and anarchy or absolute dictatorship.

In the Book of Judges there is a lesson to be learned from

the Israelites. When they had no king, no absolute authority to set the rules, "everyone did as he saw fit" (Judg. 21:25). Individuals followed their own opinions and became involved in all sorts of evil practices (Judg. 2:10–15, 19; 3:7–12; 4:1; 8:33–35; 10:3–6; 12:15–13:1). A society that rejects the Creator as its king ultimately has no valid basis for deciding what is right or wrong apart from the Bible, which lists the Creator's rules.

If God's standard is removed, what happens to the concept of "sin"? Without God's absolute laws, it crumbles. Paul told us that God gave the law so we would understand what sin was all about. If one removes the law, sin becomes an obsolete concept in most people's minds. And the Lawgiver—the Creator—becomes either (a) distant and less important, or (b) discounted as an archaic idea developed by ancient and "superstitious" peoples.

What Is Going Wrong with People and Society?

Many people are rejecting the absolute authority of God's Word simply because they are accepting a foundational belief that says they are a product of Evolution, not divine, purposeful Creation. Sadly, this anti-biblical philosophy is widely promoted through our public education systems. Increasing numbers of people are bringing their thinking into greater logical consistency with their foundational belief in Evolution. They rationalize: "If there is no Creator, who sets the absolutes, why am I still following these Christian rules [about marriage, sex, truth, ethics, etc.]? Why can't I do whatever I want to do?"

More and more, this attitude is permeating society. What will be the ultimate result? As the absolute basis of the rules and laws found in God's Word is rejected, it will be replaced by a belief that says, "Everything is relative, so everyone can have his own opinions and standards." Christian ethics will be increasingly rejected. Fewer and fewer

Modern families and society face many crucial problems and issues, including Evolutionism, promiscuity, homosexuality, divorce, abortion, and a general disregard for absolutes. To survive and flourish in these tumultuous times, Christians must understand and believe Genesis. All of what we think should be brought into subjection to the One who owns everything.

will live by Old and New Testament ideals concerning right and wrong. Marriages will dissolve and family life deteriorate. There will be a rise in abortion, homosexuality, pornography, and lawlessness of all types. People will do whatever they can get away with.

Have you noticed those things increasing today? Who could not! But, sad to say, few Christians have understood the connection between this whole foundational issue of Creation/Evolution and the great increase in the moral problems of our day. Understanding that connection is a key to understanding what's really happening in today's society.

6

Opinions and
the Christian Life

As Christians and finite humans, all of our thinking must be built on what our Creator says. We should not just add our own thinking to the biblical revelation. The Bible should be the basis for the whole of our thinking! All of what *we think* should be brought into subjection to the One who owns us and who knows everything (see 2 Cor. 10:5).

How few Christians really live this way! Opinion-oriented dogmas are destroying our churches. Because many Christians have placed their own opinions above God's Word, various churches have come to accept or at least tolerate, certain anti-biblical beliefs and practices, including homosexuality, abortion, easy divorce, situation ethics, Secular Humanist ideology, rejection of biblical absolutes, materialism, and fornication.

Tolerance of All Beliefs?

There is a great danger lurking in the general philosophy of tolerance. In Australia, a group formed and called itself Toleration, which many Christians viewed as a harmless organization with a worthy cause. Toleration's goal was to promote a tolerance of all religious ways, beliefs, and doctrines. Their major theme was "We've got to stop

A general attitude of tolerance is promoted by our public education which places a high value on personal opinion. All sorts of views are now allowed to be expressed and taught in our schools in the name of academic freedom.

being intolerant of other people's beliefs. Everyone should have a right to his or her own opinion on any matter."

Eventually the organization issued a promotional leaflet espousing this "tolerance" of all beliefs. What did the very first page contain but a detailed list of all the things they

were *against*! They said they were for a tolerance of all beliefs, yet they were *in*-tolerant of the teaching of Creationism and the absolutes of Christianity.

People who teach a tolerance of all beliefs almost invariably oppose Christianity. They cannot tolerate Christians

Ironically, this tolerant attitude usually vanishes when a student or a community member attempts to express knowledge of Christ and his Word. Knowledge of the true Creator is suppressed in our educational system. Our society is growing increasingly intolerant of the absolutes of Christianity.

saying, "Here's what's right and here's what's wrong. God says it. And so that is final." They reply, "Oh, no. We can't tolerate that. We've got to tolerate *all* beliefs."

What are they really doing? They are being intolerant of the absolutes of Christianity, because the absolutes of Christianity oppose a philosophy that says, "Everything can be done in accord with one's own opinion." It is not difficult to see that this popular philosophy is an anti-biblical way of thinking—so dangerous, in fact, that it could one day lead to the outlawing of Christianity.

Christianity and Personal Opinion

There is yet another sad aspect to the philosophy that all

people have a right to their own opinions. Not only is this being emphasized in our public education system, but it is reaching out from there and permeating all parts of our society, even our churches.

What happens today when churches address issues like abortion, homosexuality, women's role in the church, and so on? All too often, Christians are simply offering lots of different opinions, eagerly expressing their *own* ideas and beliefs. Often their leaders participate by merely summarizing these differing viewpoints and stopping short of supplying a definite conclusion about what is right or wrong according to God's Word.

The wonderful truth is that, as Christians, we can base our lives on something much more substantial than mere personal opinions! We have foundational knowledge from an Infinite Being, our Creator, to guide us. The record of this basic knowledge begins in the most foundational of all books, Genesis. Our Creator has not left us to find our own way; he has provided directions and specific principles by which to live. Christian leaders should be reminding people that God owns us and therefore sets the rules. What *he* says must be the basis for all our thinking and behavior. Our conclusions must be based on the foundation of God's Word, not on fallible human opinion!

Believing in Creation (the Genesis foundation) and submitting to the Creator's authority provides life with a strong and sure foundation. Lives that are full of hope and the power of Christ can be built on this foundation. But, like the house that

was built on the sands, a life that is founded on belief in Evolution and the changing opinions of men will inevitably end in disaster.

7

Did God Use the Evolutionary Process?

M any modern Christians have faced a disturbing and confusing problem. On the one hand, Christendom has historically believed in a literal six-day Creation, a literal created-from-dust Adam, and a time span between Creation and Christ's birth far, far shorter than millions or billions of years. On the other hand, since the beginning of this century, much of the scientific and academic world has been claiming that Evolution is a fact. Evolutionary theory has been promoted by all the major science museums, secular universities, and secular magazines.

With such so-called learned weight on the side of Evolution, many Christians understandably assumed that it *must* be true, or at least mostly so. They could see no other position to take. Not wanting to accept outright liberal theology, many Christians therefore went to their Bibles, to see how to reinterpret the Holy Scriptures in light of evolutionary interpretations of the fossils and strata.

This move to integrate Evolutionism with the Bible later proved premature. Increasing numbers of scientists, including former ardent evolutionists, eventually rose up in opposition to the dogmatic belief in Evolution and abandoned it as unproven, if not impossible. Scientific research has now produced great quantities of strong evidence against Evolution and for Creation. There are now thousands of qualified scientists who are convinced that there is no scientific proof that the evolutionary process ever took place. In their view, Evolution will eventually go down in history as the greatest myth of the century.

The purpose of this chapter is to describe the most popular theories for reinterpreting Genesis that arose prior to the advent of modern Creation Science. After each of these four theories, some basic weaknesses will be listed. However, the most serious biblical problems presented by these theories will be saved for the next chapter, which will reveal how *all* evolutionary theories (Christian or atheistic) destroy the gospel of Jesus Christ—a fact that many Christians are only now beginning to understand.

The Day-Age Theory

This idea began to be circulated in the early 1800s. Its proponents assume that the six days of Creation were not literal 24-hour–type, days. Rather, they believe one must think of the six "days" as six great ages of time during which God made our world through some evolutionary process.

Some Problems with the Day-Age Theory

1. *No death existed before Adam's sin and God's curse.* The Day-Age Theory is therefore non-biblical, for it agrees with atheistic Evolutionism in saying that death existed for millions of years before man's existence. (For further discussion, see the next chapter).

2. *The Hebrew word* yom *is translated "day" in Genesis 1 and 2.* All the uses of "yom" elsewhere in the Bible mean a literal 24-hour day when prefixed by a numerical adjective, as it is in Genesis 1 (first day, second day, etc.). The repeated reference to "evening and morning" after each of the Creation days makes it all the more clear that these are to be understood as literal *days,* not ages.

3. *The order of Creation is wrong for Evolution.* There

are many serious contradictions apparent when comparing
the order of events in Genesis with the order of events in
evolutionary theory. Here are some other examples:

Evolutionism Says	**Genesis Says**
Flowering plants and pollinating insects evolved together through mutual benefit.	Plants were created on Day 3, insects on Day 6. If these days were ages long, how did flowering plants survive?
Stars existed before the earth.	Earth existed before the stars.
Man has been carnivorous, or at least omnivorous, from the beginning.	Man was originally vegetarian. Meat-eating was not sanctioned by God until after the Flood (close to two thousand years *after* Creation).
Birds evolved from reptiles.	Reptiles ("creeping things") were created after birds.
Fishes came into existence long before the first birds.	Both fish and birds were created on the same day.
Insects evolved long before the first birds.	Insects (included in "creeping things") were created after birds.
Most of the earth's animals lived and died and became extinct long before man even existed.	The entire original animal world was created only hours before Adam, at most forty-eight hours.
The first living things were sea organisms.	Full-blown land plants were first.

Earth's plant life produced our oxygen-rich atmosphere.	Earth's life-supporting atmosphere was created before the plants.
The first fish evolved long before the first fruit trees.	Fruit trees were created before the fish.
Matter has always existed in some form.	Matter did not exist until God created it.

4. *"Evening and morning."* This phrase is repeated after every single "day" in Genesis 1! How could God have made it any more obvious that he was describing normal 24-hour days? (*Note:* According to the biblical record, during the first three days [of the earth's rotation], the source of light was not the sun, but some other "light" [Gen. 1:3], which is not explained in the text. The sun was made "to govern the day" [v. 16], which already existed. God delayed the creation of the sun till later in the week for some specific purpose—probably to symbolically give the sun lesser importance in the Creation plan. Pagans through the ages substituted the sun for the true Creator, and worshiped it as the source of all life.)

5. *God created in six literal days for a specific purpose.* God worked six days to provide an example for man to follow: the six-day work week. "Six days you shall labor and do all your work. . . . For in six days the LORD made the heavens and the earth, the sea, and all that is in them . . ." (Exod. 20:9, 11; cf. Gen. 2:2–3). Note that God personally wrote these words in stone. If—as the Day-Age Theory proposes—the word for "days" here could be translated as "indefinite eons of time," then it would be fair to translate this verse as "Six indefinite eons of time you shall labor. . . . For in six indefinite eons of time the LORD made the heavens and the earth . . ."!

6. *"Yamin" (translated "days") is used some 700 times in the Old Testament and has never proved to mean anything*

other than literal days. The word *yamin* is used in Exodus 20:9, 11—verses in which God directly refers to Creation Week days. Thus the "days" of Creation must be taken literally (*yamin* is the plural of *yom*).

The Progressive Creationist Theory

This theory likewise rejects the "days" of Creation in favor of billions of years during which God somehow used evolutionary processes so as to eventually produce the animals and plants of our present world. It is difficult to describe the details of this theory, since those who believe it have been generally unwilling or unable to provide much detail. Basically it appears that Progressive Creationists tend to accept much of Evolutionism as commonly taught (i.e., billions of years, geologic ages, "Big Bang," evolution of stars and planets, amoeba-to-man progression, etc.) However, they also believe that God created matter and set the evolutionary process in motion. Further, they generally believe that though God initially started Evolution, from time to time he intervened to create things that could not evolve on their own ("progressive creations"). Some in this group theorize that man evolved from apes and that God breathed a soul into two highly evolved ape-people ("Adam and Eve"), making them human. Others seem to believe that man was a special creation.

Some Problems with the Progressive Creationist Theory

1. *This theory has most of the same problems as the Day-Age Theory* (see the previous discussion).
2. *There is no biblical proof that God used Evolution, or that he did it over billions of years.* Quite to the contrary, there is abundant biblical and scientific evidence to indicate that God did not use an evolutionary process.
3. *Did the perfect, all-knowing, all-powerful God of love*

create a very imperfect Creation? No! The Bible indicates that his creations were fully developed, fully equipped, fully functional, "very good" (Gen. 1:31), and free of disease or suffering. Degeneration entered sometime after the Fall.

4. *The first animals were vegetarians.* Genesis 1:29–30 shows that the first land animals and birds were plant-eaters. They did not become meat-eaters until sometime after the Flood or the Fall. Evolutionists say that most early animals were carnivorous.

5. *Origin of agriculture and horticulture came early.* Evolutionism says that agriculture was not developed until relatively recently in the development of man. But the Bible says that the very first responsibility of Adam was to tend plants and garden (Gen. 2:9, 15). Cain and Abel were farmers (Gen. 4:2b).

6. *When did humans come into existence?* Evolutionists say that man did not come into being until the last 1/1500th of the earth's history. Genesis says the first man was created less than six days after the beginning of Creation.

7. *Early man was highly intelligent, and technology was developed during the lifetime of the first man, Adam.* Evolutionism says that early humans were small-brained, ape-like, primitive, and lived more or less like animals. Genesis reveals that man had a sophisticated vocabulary from the very beginning (Gen. 2:19–20, 23) and quickly developed all the basics of civilization. The origin of musical instruments, city-building, agriculture, refining of metal, tool making, and many other technologies all date back to the time of Adam and his children (Gen. 2:15; 4:2b, 17b, 20–22).

See chapter 8 for further problems with Progressive Creationism.

The Gap Theory

The Gap Theory was first proposed about 1814 in an effort to defend the Bible against attacks resulting from new interpretations of geology and the popularization of Evolutionism. The Gap Theory's basic proposition is that there is a possible time gap between Genesis 1:1 and 1:2. This idea was suggested by Dr. Thomas Chalmers of Edinburgh University, a contemporary of Charles Darwin.

Many faithful Christians accepted this theory in a genuine attempt to reject Evolution. They believed that the Creation Week was quite literal and that it did not take place millions of years ago. They theorized that the "geologic column" proposed by evolutionists could be explained by means other than Evolution (so do most Creation Scientists, who are sure that most of the column resulted from the worldwide Flood of Noah's day). Gap theorists suggested that in Genesis 1:1 God first created plants and animals and that then Satan rebelled against God and was cast to earth, causing corruption which God supposedly judged with a deluge called "Lucifer's Flood." (killing the animals and laying the sediments). The theory thus proposes that the majority of earth's fossils and fossil fuels were deposited at the end of the "gap," just *before* the Creation Week began ("first day"—Gen. 1:2).

Belief in the Gap Theory spread widely after its inclusion as a footnote in the *Scofield Reference Bible* (edition one, 1917). And the theory was further promoted and defended by Bible commentator Arthur C. Custance (*Without Form and Void,* 1970).

Some Christians eventually used the Gap Theory in a different way. Occasionally we meet Christians who have accepted many of the claims of the evolutionists and yet believe that a gap of millions of years took place between Genesis 1:1 and 1:2. They propose that "evolution" took place during this time. Their scenarios usually suggest that (a) God originally created just the simple life forms; and (b) these animals began to evolve, and the process continued for millions of years; and (c) this all took place *before* the ultimate six-day Creation Week (actually a second Creation).

In both versions of the Gap Theory, Adam and Eve were

actually created on top of an immense graveyard—an earth full of dead, buried animals.

Some Problems with the Gap Theory

1. *The Bible says that no death existed before Adam's sin and God's curse.* A main portion of this theory is therefore nonbiblical. ". . . sin entered the world through one man, and death through sin . . ." (Rom. 5:12).

2. *In context, there is no proof of any significant time gap between the first two verses of Genesis.*

3. *Was the Creation "very good"?* When God finished the Creation Week, he indicated that the entire earth and all its contents were "very good." It does not seem likely that God would use such a term if the glaring fact was that the dirt and rocks underneath Adam's feet were filled with dead, broken, smashed animals—a fact that Adam and his descendants would undoubtedly later discover. Would the God of perfection create his perfect paradise on top of a great graveyard?

4. *What evidence did Noah's Flood leave?* If the vast majority of our planet's fossils and sediments were laid during the "gap," what geologic evidence did the worldwide, cataclysmic Flood of Noah's time produce?

5. *". . . was without form and void"* (Gen. 1:2 KJV, RSV). Some scholars have suggested that the original Hebrew word translated here as "was" could also be translated as "became." However, almost all the times this word is used in the Bible it means "was." And, in examining the verse in context, there is not a single reasonable justification for translating it as "became." The original Hebrew words translated "without form and void" can be translated "formless and empty" or "unformed and unfilled" (the most accurate translation), but they *should not* be translated "ruined and desolate" or any other similar meaning that might fit the Gap Theory.

The best translation of Genesis 1:2a is: "And the earth was unformed and unfilled. . . ." (For an excellent in-depth discussion of this verse, see *Unformed and Unfilled: The Gap Theory,* by Weston W. Fields [1978: Presbyterian & Reformed Publishing.] This verse simply describes the first stage of our planet's formation. Before the creation of life, God created formless matter ["the dust of the earth"]. Then he shaped it into the form of a great revolving sphere.)

6. *If Evolution occurred during the Gap, why didn't God tell us plainly, so we would understand the fossils and strata?* If there was a "gap" during which an evolutionary process took place, why didn't the Bible make it a great deal more obvious? Should Christians struggle so hard to put Evolution into the Bible when the fit is unnatural?

7. *Misunderstanding of science and the interpretation of evidence.* Both versions of the Gap Theory were founded upon a misunderstanding of what science really is (see chapter 1) and what the evidence for the geologic column really was. They were proposed before the advent of Creation Science, which has revealed many scientific reasons to cast serious doubt on the age-dating methods of evolutionists. In addition, Creationists have revealed many scientific methods that indicate a *young* earth. Now that we understand all these things much better, we know there is no need to try to fit the strata or Evolution into a "gap" between Genesis 1:1 and Genesis 1:2.

The Genesis Allegory Theory

This theory suggests that God never meant us to take Genesis *literally*—especially the Creation story. It proposes that these chapters are not descriptions of actual historical events in any sense; they are just poetic stories, allegories designed to teach spiritual truths.

Some Problems with the Genesis Allegory Theory

1. *If the Creation and Flood records are not at all true, hasn't God been a little bit deceptive?* (For more details, see the next chapter.)

2. *How much of the rest of the Bible can be trusted?* Was Abraham literal? Were the Ten Commandments? Were Christ's miracle birth, death, and resurrection actual happenings? (Many people who believe this theory say no!)

3. *This is the position of most who accept outright liberal theology.* As the next chapter will show, any theory claiming that God used Evolution has even greater difficulties to overcome than any thus far mentioned!

How have these theories affected the thinking of Christians? Thousands of Christians can testify that once they accepted Evolution they found themselves on a path of increasing confusion and uncertainty about how to interpret Scripture. Eventually they began to question other biblical teachings. Rejection of a literal, straightforward understanding of Genesis commonly leads to a denial of the authority of the rest of Scripture, especially in light of the evidences we will discuss in the next chapter.

8

Evolutionism Destroys the Gospel

*T*his chapter is possibly the most important one *in this book.* All Christians need to clearly understand the reasons why Evolutionism harms and even destroys crucial elements of the gospel—even when God is included in the theory. Here are listed ten of Evolutionism's direct attacks on the precious gospel of Jesus Christ.

1. Origin of Death and Bloodshed

Evolutionists claim that gradual changes in the earth and its inhabitants have gone on for millions of years and that the fossils are remnants of these lost and long-ago ages. But those millions of fossils are clear evidence of death—bloodshed on a massive scale. If these animals died before Adam, the foundation of the gospel is cut at its roots (Adam sinned and corrupted paradise / Death is the penalty of that sin / As a result, sin, death, and suffering came upon not only Adam, but also the world he ruled / Christ came to save man and conquer death / Ultimately he will restore paradise). Directly denying God's Word, Evolutionism says that death is a part of life, that death and struggle have always existed and actually *led* to man's existence. (*Note:* There is much biblical and scientific evidence that most of the fossils were actually formed as a result of Noah's Flood.)

2. The Effect of Sin

If everything is evolving upward and thus getting better and better, what was God's curse all about? If Evolution is true, death and weeds and pain are nothing special, but just a natural part of life and the evolutionary process.

Most evolutionists deny the existence of a real Adam and Eve. If they are correct, our world's miserable condition (pain, unhappiness, suffering) did not result from a literal sin/Fall/curse. But, then, what *is* the cause? And why doesn't the Bible clearly reveal the true source?

3. The Purpose of Christ

The whole purpose of Christ's life and death is based on the original existence of a literal sinless paradise, a historical Adam and Eve (literally the first humans, with original bodies that need never die), an actual forbidden fruit that they ate, and a literal curse of death. Without that original sin and those literal circumstances, who would need to be redeemed?

4. Christ—Totally Good and Loving

If God used an evolutionary process to make man and all the animals, how can he be all-loving and all-good? Evolutionists believe the earth is billions of years old and that it has always been subject to earthquakes, volcanos, floods, extinction, and disease. Evolution theory suggests millions of years of harsh struggle, death, and survival of the fittest. It is a process of elimination—cold and unmerciful to the weak or deformed, with animals eating animals and brutal death over eons of time. Could even a sadist think of a more cruel and ugly way to "create" animals and man? What a horrible thing some Christians are accusing God of doing! It is shocking that some Christians defend the idea that this is the process that God set up (more or less) to bring about our world.

Our Creator's true nature is absolutely incompatible with Evolution! He said, "Blessed are the meek." Evolution generally means, "Blessed are the strong and most aggressive; the toughest shall inherit the earth."

Today we are not looking at "very good" animals in a "very good" world originally created by God (Gen. 1:31a). The world we know has obviously changed; it has fallen from its original excellence. These changes are the result of degeneration, a process set into motion by man's sin and God's curse. All creatures must cope with a world that is no longer a paradise. They now struggle to survive in a harsh, fallen, post-Flood environment. Will not *all* Creation rejoice when paradise is restored?

5. Christ—All-Powerful, All-Knowing, Absolute Perfection

If our Creator, Jesus Christ (John 1:1–3, Col. 1:16), is truly omniscient and omnipotent, he was certainly capable of creating the world in one blinding instant. So why would our all-powerful Creator purposely choose to use a process of billions of years of slow evolution? Evolutionists describe it as a great trial and error method filled with time and chance, false starts, and repeated extinctions.

How can anyone seriously suggest that Jesus Christ would set such processes into motion? What purpose would there be to it? The Creator doesn't need time, and he doesn't need to experiment. Theistic Evolutionism and Progressive Creationism take away God's glory. They strip him of his majesty and power, the very characteristics that define him. God created the original world out of his omnipotence, his glory, and his intrinsic, total perfection, which never changes.

While on the earth, the one true God frequently demonstrated the great power of his words. When he spoke, the storms were stilled instantly, not days later. Blind eyes and acute illnesses were cured totally at the very sound of his voice. His power produced immediate and complete results.

The Bible reveals that our mighty Creator specifically chose to create the world in six days, rather than in an instant or any other time period. His purpose was to create the seven-day week as a pattern for man to follow (Exod. 20:11).

6. Original Paradise

The evolutionary theory denies the existence of an original and universal paradise in which Adam and Eve were created. According to Evolutionism, life started in chaos and is gradually evolving toward greater and greater perfection. On the other hand, the Bible says the world started with excellence and order. Our world is not evolving upward; it is a fallen, degenerating world.

7. The Restoration

If Evolution is true, what kind of world can Christians look forward to in the restoration? A world of survival of the fittest? Killing, death, and mutations? Are we to be "restored" to a continuation of struggle for millions of years? To the contrary, Creation will be restored to its condition before sin and the curse. It will be the paradise described in Genesis. Evolution-contaminated theology destroys the teaching of the new heavens and the new earth.

8. The Always-Truthful Character of God

If the Bible is God's Word (as it repeatedly claims), and if Evolution is true, then God's Word is deceptive. For thousands of years, a literal, straightforward, common-sense reading of Genesis and the rest of Scripture has led millions of intelligent Christians and Israelites to believe that:

(a) The universe was created in six literal days.
(b) The earth is only thousands of years old, not millions.
  Scripture supplies a genealogy from Adam to Christ,

including great detail on ages and life spans. This surely gives some general idea of the time passed. Certainly there is no way that periods of millions of years could reasonably fit between the generations.

(c) Adam was formed directly out of dust, not from an "apeman."

Those that question the accuracy of Genesis are also questioning the veracity and knowledge of Jesus Christ. Jesus quoted from Genesis on various occasions. He accepted Genesis as historical truth. He built doctrines like marriage on the literal events of Genesis (e.g., Matt. 19:4–6). Jesus is the Way, the Truth, and the Life. He would not tell us something that was not true. Christians should believe Genesis is literally true because Jesus did! God is not a God of deception.

9. God Is in Control, and He Judges Sin

Genesis provides a record of various significant judgments by God on sin. They are evidence that God is in control and that he judges sin. If Genesis is inaccurate, as the evolutionists claim, certain stories are strongly in doubt:

(a) The Fall and God's curse (Gen. 3).

(b) The curse on Cain for committing murder (Gen. 4: 1–15).

(c) The Tower of Babel judgment (Gen. 11:1–9).

(d) The destruction of Sodom and Gomorrah (Genesis 18—19).

(e) The Genesis Flood—the single greatest of all evidences that the Creator continues to have awesome power over this earth and that he sees and punishes man's sins (Gen. 6—9).

Atheistic evolutionists say that the biblical Flood was

either a myth or a gross exaggeration. Many theistic evolutionists agree with this assessment. Such beliefs contradict the Holy Scriptures and Jesus Christ. Jesus accepted the Flood as real and worldwide (Matt. 24:37–39; Luke 17:26–27). Writers of both the New and Old Testaments accepted the Flood as literally true.

Biblical Evidences for a Worldwide Flood

(a) *The ark was truly necessary for saving Noah's family.* Otherwise, Noah could have simply migrated elsewhere for safety, instead of spending one hundred twenty years building and outfitting the largest ship ever built until modern times.

(b) *All mankind was killed.* Both the Old and New Testaments plainly teach that the Flood destroyed the planet's entire human population (probably millions of people), except for Noah's family (1 Peter 3:20, 2 Peter 3:6, etc.). Man had multiplied on the face of the earth (Gen. 6:1), and the whole planet was filled with violence and corruption (Gen. 6:11–12). Every person living today is descended from Noah (Gen. 9:1, etc.).

(c) *The ark was necessary to prevent mass extinction of animals* (Gen. 6:19–20; 7:2–4, 21–23).

(d) *The whole earth was devastated.* God said, ". . . I am surely going to destroy both them [all people] and the earth" (Gen. 6:13b; cf. 9:11; Job 12:15; 2 Peter 3:6).

(e) *All mountains were covered.* ". . . all the high mountains under the entire heavens were covered . . . . to a depth of more than twenty feet" (Gen. 7:19–20).

(f) *Noah was in the ark for over a year,* not just forty days (Gen. 7:4, 11–12, 24; 8:3–5, 13–14). The waters covered the high mountains for five months. What minor or local flood lasts that long?

(g) *God promised to never again send such a flood* (Gen. 8:21; 9:11, 15). Only once in history did God smite all living things, though local floods are common to this day. The rainbow was a sign of God's promise that such a universal flooding would never again occur (Gen. 9:13–15).

The writer of the Flood account could hardly have done a better job of plainly stating that the event was worldwide and that its effects were catastrophic.

10. Evolutionism Provides a Way to "Scientifically" Reject God

The whole idea of Evolution is based on natural processes, as distinguished from the supernatural (God, angels, miracles, divine intervention, Satan, etc.). Sir Julian Huxley, an ardent evolutionist, said: "In the evolutionary system of thought, there is no longer need nor room for the supernatural." Evolution is the most common reason people give for why they have rejected the Bible and/or God. It has been the cause of millions becoming agnostics or atheists.

Did God use Evolution? The biblical answer is clearly a resounding NO. Combining Evolutionism with Christianity has solved nothing scientifically; it has only helped Satan undermine the church. Stable, long-term faith in Christianity cannot be built in a life that is contaminated by acceptance of evolutionary theory. It is the wrong foundation. True Christian faith can flourish in peace and stability only on the foundation of the Creation account.

We urge you to help others understand why Evolutionism destroys the Gospel. Far too few Christians, including some pastors and other religious leaders, are aware of these things.

9

Sex and Marriage—
The Genesis Connection

Many areas of everyday Christian life are based on the fact that Genesis is a reliable historical record meant to be understood in a common sense, literal way. One of these areas is the marriage relationship and the family unit. If you want your marriage to work or your family to work the wonderful way God intended it to, you must clearly understand the Genesis connection. God made man and woman. God made marriage and the family unit. It is therefore vital to know his guidelines and rules. We must follow what he says, regardless of our own opinions or self-serving interests.

The Foundation of Marriage

Jesus was once asked a question about divorce, but which actually concerned marriage.

> "Haven't you read," he replied, "that at the beginning the Creator 'made them male and female,' and said, 'For this reason a man will leave his father and mother and be united to his wife, and the two will become one flesh'? . . . Therefore what God has joined together, let man not separate." (Matt. 19:4–6).

Christian belief in the institution of marriage is based on the belief that Genesis is a reliable record meant to be understood in a common sense, literal way.

Jesus was quoting from Genesis 1:27; 2:24; 5:2. Why did he quote from Genesis? Because the meaning of marriage is based on Genesis. God took dust and made Adam. He took a rib from Adam's side and made a woman. Adam knew that Eve was "bone of my bones and flesh of my flesh" (Gen. 2:23). In marriage, man and woman become *one* because they originated historically as one flesh. If this were not so historically, it would not be so now.

As the teachings of Genesis are increasingly disbelieved, ridiculed, and labeled "myth," people continue to question such Christian structures as marriage. After all, the only place marriage is ordained is in the Bible. This is where we find the basis for a monogamous marital relationship—one woman for one man.

The Issue of Homosexuality

Understanding the biblical basis for marriage makes the question of homosexuality an easy one for Christians to solve. It is not a matter of personal opinion. Homosexuality is wrong for several reasons:

1. God made Adam and Eve. Not Adam and *Steve!* He made a man and a woman, not a man and another man. And he created them with different and mutually complementary sexual parts. Sexual intercourse between males is not a natural use of the body parts that God created (Rom. 1:24–27).
2. God told mankind to be fruitful and multiply (Gen. 1:28; 9:1; 35:11). One of the primary purposes of marriage is to produce "godly offspring" (Mal. 2:15) who will honor and obey God and then themselves produce godly offspring—generation after generation.
3. The Creator severely judged and condemned the sin of homosexuality in Genesis 19. (See also Lev. 18:22; 20:13; 1 Cor. 6:9.)

If you are not a Christian and yet do believe in marriage, remember that you have no "logical" basis for it. Imagine, for instance, that you had a son who wanted to marry another man, instead of a woman. Without the Bible, you have little reason for justifying why that action would be wrong.

Stability in Marriage

It is sad that there are so many marital and family problems within our churches. Most of these problems are re-

God created Adam and Eve, not Adam and Steve. Homosexuality is not what God in his wisdom designed, and this perverse practice was condemned and judged by the Creator in Genesis 19.

lated to two important facts established by Genesis. If only more Christians would come to fully understand these simple facts and live by them, what a better world this could be. Remember that:

1. God is the Creator and therefore has the total right to control our lives. We must submit ourselves totally to his will for us.
2. God is the author of marriage and has designated certain rules for the relationship. The Creator gave man and woman different roles within marriage. All is not left up to our opinions.

The Creator's Role for the Wife

In many schools, students are taught that when you get married you remain an individual—"You've got your rights." In an effort to right societal wrongs, some feminist organizations are demanding equality in every area of life, including marriage. Again we need to ask, "What does our Creator have to say about these issues?" And this is what we find:

1. God's Word teaches that men and women *are* equal (e.g., Gal. 3:28; cf. "in his image," Gen. 1:27).
2. The wife is one with her husband, and vice versa (e.g., Gen. 2:22–24).
3. God chose not to give the wife the role of headship. The wife is to respect and obey the husband's authority (Gen. 3:16, Eph. 5:22–24). (The husband, too, has responsibilities [Eph. 5:25–32]).

This relationship was established by our Creator:

Adam was created first (surely God had a reason and purpose in this) (Gen. 2:7–8, 18–23; cf. 1 Tim. 2:13).

Physically and symbolically, God took the woman out of the man, not the man out of the woman (Gen. 2:21–23).

Though both sinned, it was Eve who deceived, not Adam (Gen. 3:20).

Eve was deceived, not Adam (Gen. 3:13).

Part of the new order established by God in the curse was: "Your desire will be for your husband, and he will rule over you" (Gen. 3:16).

The Creator's Role for the Husband (and Father)

We also need to ask what role the Creator has decreed for the husband. We find these biblical guidelines:

1. *Self-sacrificing love.* God's Word says that husbands

If you want your marriage to work the wonderful way the Creator intended, you must clearly understand the Genesis connection. God made us, man and woman, with a purpose. He made marriage and the family unit. It is therefore vital to know his guidelines and rules. And we must follow what he says regardless of our own opinions or self-serving interests.

should love their wives as Christ loved the church and gave himself for it (Eph. 5:25). Husbands are to strive to love their wives faithfully and sacrificially (vv. 26–33).

2. *Headship, including spiritual leadership.* A husband and father has the ultimate responsibility of being the spiritual head of the house and teaching the children about God (Ps. 78:1–8; Isa. 38:19; Eph. 6:4; etc.). The Bible does not mean that mothers should not be involved, but that fathers are to take the leadership role and principal responsibility.

In the majority of Christian homes today, the father's role of spiritual headship has been abdicated and left to the mother. Commonly, mothers must do the Bible readings and prayer times for the children. When fathers do not seriously accept the responsibility for spiritual headship, problems develop. For example, sons may rebel against Christianity ("If Dad doesn't think Christianity is important, neither do I"). The daughters often end up dating non-Christian men, failing to realize the true value of a godly man as head of the house. And so they end up marrying an unbeliever and getting in a mess!

Fortunately, God always has a wise purpose and loving motive in all of his rules. The biblical husband-wife relationship is *not* one where men despotically lord it over women. This is a mistaken idea that many women's liberationists have about the Bible, that it endorses a tyrannical subjection of women. Anyone who uses the biblical role-absolutes to justify one person's seeking power over another has somehow missed the whole message of Jesus Christ. The greatest law is to love one another, out of love for the God of perfect love. We all submit to one another and serve one another out of reverence and love for Christ (Eph. 5:21–33; John 13:34–35).

If you do not adopt the God-given roles and laws set out in Scripture, do not be surprised when serious problems develop in your marriage and family.

10

Parents Must Supply Strong Foundations

If children do not get the right foundation and proper leadership, Christian truths and standards will not guide their lives, and the negative effects will almost invariably extend beyond their lives and touch the next generation as well. It is a parental responsibility to transmit Christian knowledge and principles from one generation to the next. The chain tends to break down when even one father shirks his God-given duty as head of the family to learn, understand, and pass on the Christian foundations, guidelines, and behavioral examples.

Many Christian parents have learned this the hard way. As one father sadly reported, "My son rebelled against Christianity. He said, 'Why should I obey your rules?' I never thought to tell him that they weren't *my* rules. I had not grounded him in the fact that God was the Creator and that he set the rules. My son just saw the rules as my opinion, and so he decided to have his own opinion."

The Effect on Future Generations

Instruction given to or withheld from the current generation is going to affect generations to come. History has shown the results, again and again.

When the aborigines of Australia and North America were first discovered, most lacked knowledge of the Creator and his absolutes. The worship of demonic beings (evil spirits) was common. Yet, they, like us, were originally descended from godly people, such as Noah and his family and Adam and Eve, who knew much about the Creator and his rules for life. How did the aborigines lose so much crucial knowledge? Somewhere in their ancestry, their forefathers rejected God and gave themselves over to perverse and ungodly things. The same thing is happening today.

The Australian aborigines are just one of many examples. When they were first discovered, they were an anti-God people who worshiped evil spirits. They were an isolated culture using only crude stone implements. Yet, their ancestors many generations before were godly, since they descended from Noah and Adam. Former heathen cannibals in New Guinea are descendants of Noah, too—as are we all, whether Chinese, Indian, English, Jew, Arab, Christian, atheist, or hardened criminal. What has happened to cause whole groups to lose almost all knowledge of God and his truths? Somewhere in their ancestry, their forefathers rejected the Creator and became foolish in their thinking. They gave themselves over to perverse, ungodly, and degenerate things.

Noah was a godly man. How then did descendents, such as the aboriginal people and others, lose this technological knowledge and become pagan and ignorant of the true God? Some forefather in their ancestry failed to teach his children the truth and thereby rejected God. In extreme cases, it can take as little as one generation to produce a godless culture.

What is going to happen in more advanced nations such as our own that have had strong roots in Christianity, but have now abandoned them? During this century, generations of young people have been sent through a public education system that does not allow teaching about God or the Bible. Most television programs, magazines, and music have become *un*-godly, ignoring the reality of God and his relevance to daily life. Schools have been teaching children that they are primates, just highly advanced animals who reached a high level of development through a gradual survival-of-the-fittest evolutionary process based on chance.

As we speak in public schools we are often shocked to find students totally ignorant of the five most important events in history—Creation/Fall/Flood/Babel/Christ. We repeatedly find students who know nothing more about "Jesus Christ" than that they are a pair of commonly used swear words! Is it any wonder that godlessness and moral laxity are becoming so prevalent? We are producing a godless generation.

A major reason why there are so many problems in Christian families today is that fathers have not taken their spiritual-leadership role seriously. What an awesome responsibility Christian parents have. If we do not give our children the right foundation, the Christian structure is not going to stand, and "civilized" society itself will fall.

In many public schools today, entrance is freely given to all sorts of questionable beliefs and theories, including the philosophies of the New Age movement. But when scientists and teachers attempt to present valid scientific evidence against

Clothing and Modesty

Consider but one practical reason for fathers to train their children in the foundations of Genesis. Why do we wear clothes? To stay warm? To shield our bodies from the

Evolution, they are frequently prohibited. Our education system is creating a godless generation; millions of people are totally lacking foundational knowledge of their Creator, Redeemer, and Judge. The sad result is becoming all too obvious.

sun? To be fashionable? There can be many reasons. But the most basic reason for clothing is a moral one: *God gave clothes because of sin.* Where do we go to find that? The Book of Genesis! The meaning of anything can be found in

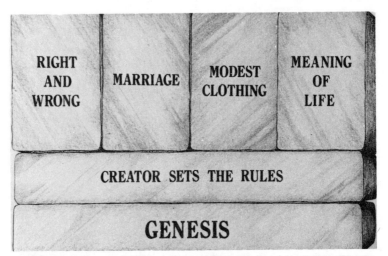

| RIGHT AND WRONG | MARRIAGE | MODEST CLOTHING | MEANING OF LIFE |

CREATOR SETS THE RULES

GENESIS

Because Christians have the Genesis foundation, they have a basis for a Christian world-view. They understand that the Creator has a rightful authority over their lives. They can understand what marriage, sex, and a standard for clothing are all about. It is vitally important that children clearly understand the underlying biblical reasons for what parents teach.

its origins. There is a "Genesis Connection" regarding clothing—truths that parents should teach their children:

1. *The original world was excellent and without sin.*

2. *Clothes were not originally necessary.* Before the fall, Adam and Eve were naked and felt no shame (Gen. 2:25). As long as they were totally innocent of any sin, there was nothing inherently wrong in nakedness.

3. *Man rebelled against God.* Sin came into the world.

4. *Sin distorts nakedness.* Sin distorts everything! As sinful creatures before a pure and holy God, Adam and Eve immediately saw their nakedness in a much different light (Gen. 3:7, 10).

5. *God gave clothes.* As a result of the entrance of sin, God gave Adam and Eve garments of animal skin and clothed them (Gen. 3:21). This was the first blood sacrifice as a covering for their sin, a beautiful symbol of the redemption to come.

6. *Moral purpose of clothes.* The covering was given for a

moral purpose related to the new sin nature of man. The need became all too obvious as new generations were born into the world. More immediately, the skins covered Adam and Eve symbolically before their Holy God. Fashion was not the original purpose of clothes, and neither was warmth. Fossil evidence indicates that the pre-Flood climate probably remained close to Edenic perfection—not too hot or too cold. There is no scriptural evidence to the contrary.

7. *Lust is a sin and leads to worse sins.* In the New Testament, men are given a specific warning: if a man lusts after a woman in his heart, he commits adultery in his heart (Matt. 5:28).

8. *The sexual nature is distorted by sin.* Why does the Bible single men out for the above warning? If you are a man, you know! Men respond sexually to a woman's body relatively easily. Men were created that way. It was to be a normal and beautiful response to one woman (his wife) in a wonderful relationship. But sin has distorted that, and now men have a special problem with what is called lust. (Many girls do not fully understand how what they wear can so easily affect men.) If fathers (and mothers, too) do not clearly explain this, daughters sometimes end up learning the hard way.

9. *Parents have the right to make the final decision about their children's behavior.* That is their role and responsibility. "Children, obey your parents in the Lord: for this is right" (Eph. 6:1; cf. Prov. 6:20; Col. 3:20).

10. *God is the Creator, and so he has the right to set the rules.* Fathers need to explain all these things, especially to their daughters. What women wear (or don't wear) can easily put a stumbling block in a man's way and tempt him into committing adultery in his heart. Even young children need to understand that selecting clothing is not just a matter of the fashions of the day. They must take into account the moral reason for clothing. Understanding our sexual nature and how sin has distorted nakedness gives us

a basis for determining a basic standard of clothing appropriate for the environment in which we live.

And, of course, there is a need for modesty in dress and behavior among men, too. God gave garments to both Eve *and* Adam. Although the emphasis here has been on female deportment, a man is no less guilty if he *succumbs* to the "second look" (see Job 31:1).

11

The Destruction of Society

W hat has evolutionary teaching done to modern man's thinking? For millions of children and parents, it has fashioned their whole world-view. It has influenced their beliefs about man's purpose and destiny. It has affected life's choices and actions. Christians must realize the truth and implications of this unfortunate trend. What you believe about where you came from affects your view of life and your view of your fellowman.

The Basic World-View of the Christian

Because Christians have the Genesis foundation, they have a basis for a Christian world-view. They understand that the Creator has rightful authority over their lives. They know that every person is equal before God. They recognize that we are all sinners and, as God measures things, that no one is really much better than anyone else. More specifically, they know what marriage and sex are all about. They understand, too, why they should have a standard for clothing.

Christians understand that sin is the source of this world's pain and unhappiness. But they know that there is a divine purpose in history and that all the wrongs of this world will one day be righted. They know that the Creator will one day restore Creation to its original excellence. Christians look forward to a bright and joyful eternal life, knowing that this sad, corrupt world is not all there is!

The Basic World-View of the Secular Humanist

Secular Humanism is one of the most popular world-views of our age. It is founded on belief in Evolution as fact and includes the idea that God does not exist (Humanist Manifestos I & II). Secular Humanists believe that people are just a product of chance and that "science" has proven the Bible wrong. They therefore conclude that there is no Creator who owns us and that humans must rely totally on their own reasoning in this world to reach an opinion about correct behavior.

As Secular Humanists bring their actions and thoughts into greater and greater consistency with these beliefs, various dangerous ramifications develop. Each of the following comments is quite logical if one rejects Genesis (and the rest of the Bible), as so many people have done:

"This life is the only one you're going to get, so enjoy it while you can. Do what makes you happy."

"Why worry about trying to figure out what is right and wrong if there is no ultimate, eternal meaning to life anyway."

"We have a right to make our own rules and guidelines about living in this world. Why not do whatever you can get away with?"

"There is no reason to feel guilty about anything done with our sexual drive. There is nothing morally wrong with homosexuality, fornication, or adultery."

"There are no moral absolutes."

"Because we are just animals anyway, what's wrong with aborting unwanted babies? Abortion is a great thing for women. Why should they have to suffer distressing consequences for their little mistakes and accidents?"

"You have a right to decide how to live, and you have a right to put your own interests first. Never forget old Number One."

As the Genesis foundation is increasingly removed from society and replaced with evolutionary philosophy, we can expect to see anti-God actions increasing and Christian ethics decreasing. The more people accept evolutionary concepts, the more their world-view will logically adjust to fit that basically atheistic belief system. We can expect to see all the absolutes collapsing. And we do! All around us.

In a sense, however, it is not Evolutionism that is the root cause of the problems in our society. The ultimate cause of these problems has always been sin, man's disobedience. Ever since the Garden of Eden, people have been rebellious in one way or another. Some ignore the Creator by not taking his authority seriously. Others reject God as the true ultimate source of all life and power and/or his relevance for today's living. Some arrogantly deny God's very existence in the past, present, or future.

Throughout man's history, the true nature of God has been rejected on the basis of many different belief systems (e.g., atheism, belief in other gods, belief that the universe and the gods evolved, worship of Satan or evil spirits, worship of animals, stars, or other "natural" entities). Once the Western cultures were predominated by the light of Christian truths, but now Secular Humanism has taken control. Today, millions of people are using Evolution as a "scientific" justification for rejecting the Creator and his Word. Whenever a society rejects the true Creator's authority and laws, immorality will inevitably increase.

Abortion—The Evolution Connection

Although few Christians realize it, the increasing acceptance of abortion has gone hand in hand with the increasing popularity of evolutionary theory. Abortion

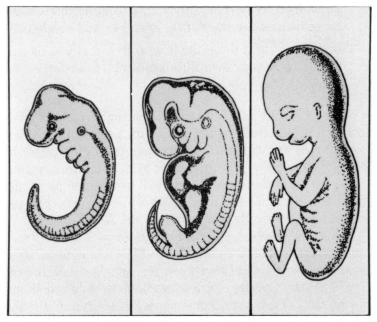

This is one of many examples of evolutionary theories which have been used to justify immoral acts. Millions were taught that the human embryo retraces the various stages of animal evolution, as it develops: protozoan to fish to reptile to man. Although this theory was a fraud from the beginning, it has sometimes been used to promote abortion—justifying it as the killing of an animal, not a human.

has been promoted by Evolutionism in at least three ways:

1. *Evolutionism has taught that humans are just animals,* one of many other creatures living on an insignificant speck of a planet in a vast universe. All too many abortions have been justified by reasoning that crudely implies: "You get rid of spare cats and other animals, so why not get rid of unwanted children? They're just animals, too, so it doesn't really matter."

2. *Evolutionism has removed the moral basis for obeying the Ten Commandments.* If there is no God—at least not the personal God of the Bible—"thou shalt not kill" and other such divine commands are just arbitrary rules written by the ancient Israelites. Thus people claim an absolute right to do what they want to with their own body, including the contents of their body.

3. *Evolutionism once taught that human embryos are not human beings.* Many people still believe the following erroneous evolutionary view once widely taught in schools. A scientist named Ernest Haeckel developed a theory that said the human embryo retraces the various stages of Evolution (embryonic recapitulation: "Ontogeny recapitulates phylogeny"). This theory proposed that the embryo goes through a protozoan stage, a jellyfish stage, and later reaches a fish stage, where it has gill slits. And so it goes on—until it finally *becomes* human.

Millions of people were taught this theory as fact, though it was actually a fraud from the beginning since Haeckel presented altered, misleading, and misinterpreted evidence. Some of the key details of his embryo drawings were wrong. Yet, how many people know this? Tragically, one can occasionally still find this theory being taught or implied in schools and universities. Some "pro-choice" advocates and abortion clinics have used this evolutionary concept to make abortion more palatable: "We're not cutting up a baby; it's just a fish or a jellyfish. It's not human; it's just tissue."

Our increasingly immoral society is an outward expression of the rejection of God and his absolutes in more and more naked ferocity. Millions of babies are being killed before birth—cut up and sucked out in bits and pieces. And it is legal by secular standards. Is not our society degenerating into godless barbarism, just as so many other God-rejecting cultures have done? God allows us no "choice" regarding the sanctity of human life.

Racism—The Evolution Connection

Racism has often been rationalized on the basis of evolutionary theory. Many schools have taught that different races had evolved to different levels, with some not as advanced as others. The full title of Darwin's most famous book was *On the Origin of Species by Means of Natural*

Tragic racism has been rationalized on the basis of false evolutionary theories. Many schools once taught that, having evolved from ape-like animals, some races were not as highly evolved as others—more primitive, less desirable, and even subhuman. Under this belief, some whites blithely exterminated Australian aborigines, and Adolf Hitler attempted to exterminate the Jews.

Selection or The Preservation of Favoured Races in the Struggle for Life. During the great rise of Evolutionism, many scientists held very racist beliefs (much documentation can be found in *Outcasts from Evolution: Scientific Attitudes of Racial Inferiority, 1859–1900,* John S. Haller, Jr. [Urbana: University of Illinois Press, 1971]).

Many white settlers in Australia believed the aborigines were primitive sub-humans and thus incapable of understanding the white man's technology and ways. And so they were thought to be a threat. This is one of the reasons why some settlers in the state of Tasmania shot every aborigine they could find, with little remorse.

Europeans believed similar racist concepts about the blacks of Africa and the Mongolian (or Mongoloid) races. Non-whites were thought to be less evolved. According to evolutionist Stephen J. Gould, this is one of the reasons why the term *mongoloid* was later applied to certain mentally defective people. Such misguided ideas were just another one of many sad results of teaching Evolution as undeniable fact in our public-education system.

The particularly barbaric racism of Hitler was strongly connected to belief in Evolution. In various ways, the Nazis attempted to propel and experiment with the human evolutionary process. There were attempts to breed a superior race and efforts to "purify" the human gene pool by exterminating "undesirable" races and individuals. In many ways, Nazism lived by the evolutionary motto: "survival of the fittest." Hitler believed it was the destiny and right of Nordic Caucasians to dominate the weaker races.

To understand the true nature of races and their ultimate source, one must refute the racist claims of some evolutionists by looking again to the events of Genesis, where we find the following truths:

1. *Adam and Eve were the ancestors of all mankind.* They were created with a complete genetic code that allowed for diversity.

2. *Man started out perfect.* We have every reason to assume that Adam and Eve had perfect bodies and superb minds with extremely high I.Q.s. Next to the original Adam, we are all surely inferior and degenerate specimens!

3. *The Fall distorted all mankind.* Sin, evil, and rejection of God spread through all humanity through Adam. After the Fall, the original excellence of Creation was no longer maintained by God. In the thousands of generations that followed, mutation and physical degeneration began to change man's chromosomes and multiply the undesirable attributes.

4. *The Flood changed the geography and geology of the world.* This event produced areas of the world where people could become isolated for hundreds and thousands of years.

The various great environmental changes left in the wake of the Flood almost certainly affected man physically in the generations that followed Noah and resulted in the ultimate extinction of many animals, including dinosaurs. Some of the significant side effects were loss of the originally perfect soils, atmospheric changes, extreme climates, increased exposure to harmful cosmic and solar radiation, etc.).

5. *The Tower of Babel divided humanity.* This event is very important for understanding the origin of distinctive racial characteristics. The immediate confusion of languages resulted in a strong and long-lasting division among man, politically, geographically, and culturally. It instantly divided humanity into very diverse language groups. Many of these people then moved away from Babel and out into all areas of the earth. Some of the groups became isolated by distance, mountain ranges, and oceans. Each isolated group was therefore left with a reduced potential gene pool. Since children acquire the physical characteristics of their parents, long-term inbreeding within these isolated groups caused unique characteristics in each to become more and more emphasized in following generations. These features included nose shape, eye shape and color, hair type, lip shape, degree of skin pigmentation, body size, and skull shape. Cultural differences also naturally developed due to isolation. Spiritual degeneration in some groups likewise increased, and in some regions whole generations lost almost all knowledge of God and their true origins.

Communism—The Evolution Connection

It is well known that the state religion of the U.S.S.R. and other Communist nations is atheism. The whole Communist ideology is justified in a view of origins that says, "There is no God." Evolution is used to defend and promote atheism in these countries. Karl Marx, the father of political Communism, wanted to dedicate his famous book *Das Kapital* to Charles Darwin, the father of modern Evolutionism.

A university lecturer in Australia has reported his experiences with Communist students in China. In their culture, he said, when a Communist student becomes a Christian, the first thing people usually ask is, "So you have given up Darwin?" They automatically equate becoming a Christian with rejecting Evolutionism.

Other Ways in Which Evolutionary Teaching Can Destroy Society

As "the Genesis connection" is increasingly removed from modern society and replaced by belief in Evolution and Secular Humanism, we can logically expect various tragic results:

1. Decrease in marriage (fewer people will bother with it).
2. Decrease in the work ethic. Genesis is where man was told to work. It also reveals why work has become hard—a result of sin and God's curse.
   God's curse.
3. Fewer men will act as the heads of families. Without a Genesis base, people will question why a man should be the head of the house.
4. More people will question the value of life. After all, if God didn't create life and we are here by chance, what value is life anyway—especially when life is unhappy?
5. Increase in suicides, "mercy killings," and euthanasia.
6. Increase in promiscuity.
7. Increase in all forms of self-indulgence.
8. Increase in pornography.
9. Increase in abortions.
10. Increase in public nudity. The only moral basis for clothing and modesty is founded in Genesis.
11. Decreasing ability of juries and judges to agree on verdicts. What basis do they have for deciding right

As belief in Genesis is increasingly removed from modern society and replaced by belief in Evolution and Secular Humanism, we can logically expect the vigorous growth of many ungodly practices.

and wrong and punishments if there are no clear definitions of "criminality"?

12. Increase in rape and sexual abuse of children. The attitude will be that sexual desires are a natural part of our animal instincts. "If a person can get what he wants, why not take it?"

13. Increase in homosexuality. The only basis for forbidding it is in the Bible, beginning with Genesis.

14. Increase in theft and violence. If there is no God, what is "morality," except whatever you want to make it? All becomes relative.

15. Decreasing respect for law. Increasing anarchy.

16. Increasing government control. *Examples:* Questioning parents' rights over their children; government legislation to "protect" children from their parents (some of which is justified due to rampant child abuse by parents' acting out their ungodly thoughts

and attitudes); increasing government control over education; stifling of religious liberty.

17. Increasing rule of Communism and other atheistic and authoritarian governments.

Christians, Wake up!

These things are exactly what we are seeing in today's society. People are building their lives upon Evolutionism, which is a false view of origins. And they are behaving more in accord with this view. Our declining society is an outward expression of an inward rejection of the Creator. And our freedoms are being eroded as Christianity is being slowly eliminated.

Christians may wake up one day to find Christianity outlawed. And many will wonder how and why it happened, not knowing that the blame lies with themselves. They did not stand firm on the truth of God's Word.

For too long, many Christians and church denominations have either ignored the inroads of Evolutionism or compromised on its theories. They have not understood the philosophic, theologic, and scientific problems they were creating by taking these positions, especially the devastating effects that would ultimately result for society and the Christian faith.

12

How to Win the Battle

There are many problems that concerned Christians would love to solve triumphantly—pornography, homosexuality, drugs, abortion, materialism, increasing crime, lax morality, and many others. Unfortunately, it often seems that the church is losing these battles. Why? There are many reasons, but the most basic factor is that so few Christians understand where the real battleground lies.

Imagine two castles. One is called Secular Humanism, and its foundation is Evolution. At the top of this castle are flags representing some of the various issues, all the ultimate and natural result of the Secular Humanist belief system and world-view. The second castle is called Christianity. It represents the church, and its foundation is Creation, representing Christ, our Creator and Redeemer, and Genesis 1–11—God's most foundational written record.

There are people with cannons in each castle. The Secular Humanists have their guns aimed at the Creation foundation, for they know that the castle of Christianity will collapse if its foundation is destroyed.

In the meantime, what are Christians doing?

1. *Shooting at each other.* They are backbiting and infighting within the church, tolerating denominational

Today, Christianity is at battle with Secular Humanism. Christianity stands on the foundation of Creation. Secular Humanism has been built on the theory of Evolution—without which, it would collapse.

On top of the Humanist castle are various flags, representing issues, such as: the legalization of abortion, homosexuality, euthanasia (killing the old and unproductive), legalized pornography, rejection of prayer in schools, and so on. All these are the ultimate and natural outgrowths of the Secular Humanist belief system and world-view.

How are most Christians fighting the battle? By shooting at the flags! Secular Humanists, on the other hand, are effectively blasting the foundation out from beneath us!

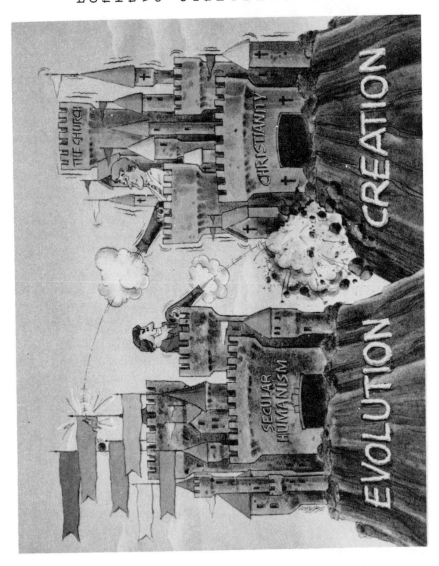

bickering, and expressing critical attitudes toward religious leaders.

2. *Shooting into nowhere.* Although anxious to help, they lack direction and make lots of noise, but contribute nothing significant to the battle.

3. *Shooting at their own foundation.* This includes promoting belief in theistic Evolutionism.

4. *Shooting at the individual issues.*

5. *Aiming at the other castle* by trying to chip away at Secular Humanism.

Aiming *Only* at the Issues

In our illustration, Christians are not effectively fighting either Secular Humanism or the issues involved. Nor are they effectively defending themselves against the dangers. It is not good enough to just fight the symptoms of godlessness. If we don't fight at the foundational level, we will lose both the individual battles and the entire war in the long run.

If we do not aim at the foundation of Secular Humanism—Evolutionism—but simply at the issues, what will happen? We may minimize or eliminate abortion or pornography by getting the laws changed, but what will be the ultimate result? People will still be taught that Evolution is factual, and they will still become Secular Humanists in one form or another. When the next Creation-rejecting generation comes along, they will probably just change the laws back again! We must fight these issues at a foundational level. That is where the real battle is.

Join the Battle

Creation/Evolution is not just a side issue! It is one of the most fundamental and important issues of today. If Christians do not grasp what the foundational issues are, there is not going to be long-term success in changing or evangelizing society.

There is an ongoing war in society: Christianity versus Secular Humanism. But, at a foundational level, it is really Creation versus Evolution. As the Secular Humanists blast away at Creationism, belief in God as Creator and belief in Genesis as God's Word are being lost in society. The foundation of Christianity is being destroyed. Christians must rebuild this foundation and effectively attack evolutionary theory, exposing it as wrong and unscientific.

13

The Serpent in the Church

Christians are being bombarded with evolutionary propaganda by the media and the schools. Yet, as Christianity's very foundations are being eroded away, how few Christians react against it!

Imagine the following scene: Inside your church you notice a large, ominous snake, roaming freely but undetected by others. You see it moving stealthily about the pews, unnoticed. Imagine watching it stalk the children of the church as they play. Would you not want to shout a warning to the children and the congregation?

This is the situation faced by Creationists. They see Evolution, the serpent of Satan, stalking the church and its children and understand the critical danger. Yet so few Christians take any notice. Or if they do, they show no interest in helping Creationists sound a loud and clear warning. Even our children's current delight with dinosaurs is being used to lead them away from the truths of God's Word. Evolutionism is defeating the church while—despite all the obvious damage—few Christians have any idea that the serpent is among them! Some are even unknowingly responsible for carrying the serpent into the church and setting it loose. The Great Deceiver has blinded many eyes.

Evolutionism in Our Christian Schools

Tragically, it is all too easy to find Christian school-teachers, professors, and administrators in our country and elsewhere who are woefully uninformed about Creationism and the Genesis truths. As a result, the church is training pastors, missionaries, and teachers who know little or nothing about the evidence for Creation or the foundational importance of Genesis.

We recently learned of a school that was teaching Evolutionism in Africa. The only teacher in the school who taught Creationism was rebuked by the other teachers and asked to stop. The tragic irony is that the school is run by a well-known American evangelical mission organization! And the school is for the children of missionary evangelists! Is it any wonder that the church is floundering and evangelism efforts often fall flat?

Many Christians are totally unaware of what is going on within their own denomination's schools and seminaries. Many faithful parents have scrimped and saved to send their child to a Christian college, trying to get them properly educated in historic, *biblical* truths. Tragically, many of those church-sponsored colleges and seminaries are teaching Evolutionism to one degree or another. Our very own Christian schools are sowing doubt about God's Word! As a result, it is not terribly uncommon to see enthusiastic Christian young people enter seminary and then lose their faith, or at least their enthusiasm.

An alarming number of the next generation of pastors, Sunday-school teachers, lay leaders, and missionaries have been taught that evolutionary theory is acceptable and compatible with Christianity. This is an extremely serious error—a foolish and needless compromise that is poisoning the church from within. Not only are people losing faith in the Bible's accuracy, but the truth of the gospel message is being lost!

History has shown that Christian colleges and seminaries that accept Evolution as factual invariably move closer and closer to full liberalism over the years, unless strong counteraction is taken. Even such ranking secular schools as Harvard and Yale were once strong *Christian* schools. (Harvard was named after a Puritan minister.) As acceptance of Evolutionism spread within their faculties, more and more liberal theology was accepted by schools originally founded by the church. Eventually all Christian truths were buried, and there was no more point to retaining a Christian label. And so they became totally secular.

Far too many Christian colleges are following this same path today. They are accepting Evolution and rejecting belief in a literal Genesis. For public-relations purposes, many attempt to cover up this fact. They may still use such words as *Creation, Creationist,* and *literal,* but they pervert their normal, commonly understood meanings with novel new definitions and qualifications. Other Christian schools are farther down the road toward complete and open acceptance of Evolution, and so they make no pretext about their beliefs. Some are even sponsoring and warmly welcoming anti-Creationist speakers.

False Accusations

Some Christians are so uninformed (or misinformed) about Creationism that they have made the incredible accusation that it is the Creationists who are introducing division and confusion into the church. But Creationists who believe that Genesis is accurate are *not* promoting some new and bizarre idea. Rather, they are merely affirming age-long historical beliefs of God's people. They are standing firm on the Word of God and defending its accuracy. Few Creationists are departing from the Word of God. It is the theistic evolutionists and so-called Progressive Creationists who have rejected the historic beliefs and doctrines of Christianity. It is they who are helping spread a gospel-destroying heresy within the church and thus causing division and confusion.

On the Mission Field

Evolutionary teaching has spread throughout the entire world. It is found in the grass-hut schools of remote villages and in highly educated Oriental nations like Japan, where it is acknowledged as one of the greatest obstacles to evangelism. It is in all Communist countries and most Arabic lands. We know of no nation where Evolution has not become a hindrance to soul-winning.

In China, Christianity was once widely accepted, due to years of fervent mission work from the West. But eventually a number of new missionary recruits were supplied from mainline Protestant denominations with seminaries contaminated with evolutionary philosophy. These new missionaries expressed their belief in Evolution and refuted the inerrancy of Scripture. As Chinese confidence in Christianity was undermined, the Chinese people were readied for the coming of atheistic Communism.

Christian, Open Your Eyes!

Christians must open their eyes to what is happening and then take action. God's people must protect Christianity's Genesis foundation and actively oppose false evolutionary teachings. It is thrilling to see what can happen when Christian schools and denominations take a stand on this foundational issue!

14

The "Creation Evangelism" Solution!

Why is the gospel so often falling on deaf ears? The teaching of Evolution has undeniably become a major reason why millions are now unreceptive to the gospel of Jesus Christ. Generations have been deceived into believing that Genesis is inaccurate. Evolutionary thought is so firmly entrenched that many view Christianity with absolute contempt and incredulity. The reasoning is: "How can anyone possibly believe the Bible when it says God created Adam and Eve, and we know that isn't true! Evolution is a proven fact of science."

Such nay-sayers are convinced that Christianity is unscientific, outdated, false, and irrelevant. For them, science has "proved" there is no need for God and that all is explainable by natural means. So people live sad, degenerate lives—ignoring the Creator who loves them and who so eagerly wants to provide them with true happiness and eternal salvation.

Thus, much of our world has become highly secular and un-Godly, lacking all knowledge of God. It is not uncommon to find public-school students who are as ignorant as unreached, primitive natives when it comes to the subject of Jesus Christ or Creation. This is shocking, but only too true. Despite great expenditures of money and talent, many evangelism efforts these days are producing disappointingly small results, not reaping the great numbers of souls as was common in earlier centuries.

Paul's Effective Method for Preaching the Gospel

How did the apostle Paul approach such people with the Good News of the gospel? Being a well-educated man, he discerned a fundamental difference in their background knowledge. This difference had a remarkable effect on how individuals first received the preaching of Christ's death and resurrection. To the Jews, this message was often a stumbling block, yet basically understandable. But to the Greeks (Gentiles), it usually sounded like utter foolishness (1 Cor. 1:23).

Why did the Jews and the Greeks receive the same message so differently?

The Jews already had the Creation foundation. They were familiar with the nature of God and his authority. The foundations of the gospel were already understood (Creation/the Fall/etc.). But the Greeks knew almost nothing of this foundational information, such an important key to understanding the rest of the gospel message.

The Greeks basically believed in a form of Evolution. They thought that both the gods and man evolved. Paul took note of their beliefs and their ignorances. To establish a basis for the cross, he knew that he had to eliminate their incorrect foundational beliefs and replace them with the right foundation: Creation. When dealing with the "Greeks" at Mars Hill, Paul began by establishing the foundation that God was Creator:

> "For as I walked around and observed your objects of worship, I even found an altar with this inscription: TO AN UNKNOWN GOD. Now what you worship as something unknown I am going to proclaim to you. *The God who made the world and everything in it is the Lord of heaven and earth* and does

not live in temples built by hands. And he is not served by human hands, as if he needed anything, because *he himself gives all men life and breath and everything else. From one man [Adam] he made every nation of men, that they should inhabit the whole earth. . ."* (Acts 17:23–26, italics added).

Our Modern Society of "Greeks"

Years ago, most Western societies were much more like that of the Jews. People had the Genesis foundation and almost everyone was familiar with the Creation account, whose accuracy was seldom questioned. People also knew of the Flood judgment and generally accepted that it had produced the fossils and sedimentary rocks. Genesis was taught in universities and elementary schools, and the Bible was read as a textbook. Evangelists could come in and share the message of the cross and get a tremendous response. But there has been a change! And few in the church have noted its significance.

Our society is no longer like that. Our education system is producing generations of "Greeks," ignorant of basic truths about God and about man's beginnings. And so the message of the cross often falls on deaf ears. Today, the Creation foundation is all but eroded away in Western society and replaced with an evolutionary base.

Most current evangelistic thrusts in America really only reach those with some sort of Bible knowledge or church background—people with some basic understanding of Christianity. The "pagans" are hardly being reached at all.

The Sower and the Seed

Think about Christ's parable of the sower and the seed. When the seed fell on rocky and thorny ground, it could not grow. It could flourish only when it fell upon prepared soil. The seed represents the message of the cross. We Christians are to be the sowers, but we must understand that much of

our seed is falling on the thorny, rocky ground of evolutionary philosophy. To be successful in reaching the un-Godly, we must get to work, clearing away those rocks and thorns and trees so the ground will be prepared to receive the seed.

A method has been developed to do just that. Creation evangelism first clears the way and then plants the seed. It provides scientific evidence to show that Genesis and the

In the parable of the sower and the seed, Christ reminded us that seeds need prepared soil to grow well and blossom. The seeds represent the message of the cross. We Christians are to be the sowers. But to be effective, the hearts of the unsaved must be adequately prepared to receive the message, otherwise the seed will not flourish.

rest of the Bible is not a collection of fairy tales. It shares the foundational information of Genesis and tells the Creation story carefully and accurately. In short, it explains the foundations of Christianity before proceeding to the rest of the gospel.

A small but increasing number of mission organizations are excited about this approach and are putting it to work.

Today, much of our seed is falling on minds blocked by the thorns and rocks of evolutionary beliefs and philosophy. To be successful, we must get to work, clearing away those obstacles and preparing the way for the gospel.

Like a sower with a garden hoe, we can first help clear people's minds of false theories and misconceptions by revealing the strong scientific evidence supporting the Bible. Then we can share the simple, but foundational, information which so many people sadly lack today: the account of creation, man's sin, and so on. Hearts will be far better prepared to receive the Good News of the cross and resurrection, having first understood its foundation.

The response has been excellent! Those who have applied only part of the technique now want to go all the way.

New Tribes Mission has been using a Creation evangelism approach for some years now and with great success. Formerly, topical preaching methods were used to try to win tribal peoples of New Guinea and similar areas. The missionaries usually preached the Gospels of Matthew, Mark, Luke, and John. But the results were frequently disappointing. Converts were few and far between. New believers often lost faith and returned to their former pagan ways.

The organization now trains its missionaries to build a strong foundation before proceeding to the rest of the Christian structure and belief system. They call it the "chronological panoramic approach" or simply "chronologic teaching." Now, when they come to a new tribe, evangelists start by sharing Genesis and its foundational knowledge. They explain who God is, the original paradise, where sin came from, where death came from, and so on. Only after many weeks or even months do they begin to share the Good News of Christ's birth, death, and resurrection.

The results have been marvelous! And other missions are following their example. Converts are now standing the test of time, simply because they finally understand the basis of the Christian faith. Strong foundations are being laid and built upon.

How to Use Creation Evangelism

All Christians can have a part in defeating the lies of Evolutionism. Don't be hoodwinked into thinking you have to be a scientist or theologian to do so. *Evolution is not science; it is a belief!* You don't need a science degree to combat it. The presentation of many available and easy-to-understand scientific evidences can help break down barriers. People who would not previously listen will begin to open their minds and think about Christianity more seriously. Some of the suggested areas to discuss with those who accept Evolution are:

1. Evidence that God exists, including the evidence from design.
2. What science really is, and what it can and cannot prove.
3. Evidences of the scientific emptiness of Evolutionism.
4. Evidence for how dinosaurs fit into the Bible and history.
5. Evidence for Noah's Flood.
6. Evidence that man has not evolved from a "lower" order.
7. And so on. . . .

Christians must also present the clear story of Genesis and the whole gospel. One should not assume that most people already know the details and understand what the record means. Even many regular church attenders do not understand. Millions of people have a distorted, inaccurate idea of what Genesis says. People frequently do not understand that the environment, the animals, and man are all following a path of degeneration. The world is not evolving upward; it is degenerating downward. Everything began in excellence when God created it.

People commonly make the mistake of misinterpreting the problems around them—suffering, carnivorous animals, parasites, disease, harsh climates—and assuming that this is the world God created. They often doubt God's goodness because these problems exist. What they fail to understand is that our planet is a fallen, degenerated world that no longer reflects the excellence that God first created. We live in a world full of the evidence of (a) man's sin, and (b) God's righteous and wise judgments on sin (the Fall, the curse, the confusion of languages, the Flood, and so on). And the Creator has provided a wonderful way to ultimately restore Creation and save those who turn from sin: the redemption offered us by Jesus Christ.

Some Tools of Creation Evangelism

1. *The Genesis Solution* film or video. Uninformed Christians can be reached through this effective 45-minute motion picture in which Ken Ham personally shares the basic information of this book. Includes humorous animation.

2. *Share this book* with friends. Donate copies to pastors, teachers and libraries.

3. *The Genesis Record* by Dr. Henry M. Morris. Probably the best available verse-by-verse commentary on Genesis. Written by a scholar who well understands Creation evangelism and is extremely knowledgeable about scientific evidence that supports the Book of Genesis. (Publisher: Baker Book House.)

4. *The God Who Is Real: A Creationist Approach to Evangelism and Missions* by Dr. Henry M. Morris. This concise book shares more important details about Creation evangelism. It can help pastors, evangelists, students, and laypeople learn to be more effective for Christ. It illustrates how to use Creationism in evangelism and includes a good summary of the scientific evidences for Creation, the historical evidences for the deity of Christ, and the logical evidences for the unique authority of the Christian gospel of salvation. (Publisher: Baker Book House.)

5. *Evolution: The Lie* by Ken Ham. Hardcover book that goes into greater depth on the issues discussed in *The Genesis Solution* and includes additional information and the author's many interesting personal experiences. (Publisher: Master Books.)

6. *The Great Dinosaur Mystery and the Bible* by Paul S. Taylor. One of the most frequently heard Creation/Evolution questions is "What about dinosaurs; how do they fit into the Bible?" This richly illustrated hardcover book provides answers and is great for both young people and adults. The text uses the techniques of Creation evangelism to show the way of salvation. (Produced by the Films For Christ Association; publisher: Master Books.)

7. *Creationist Speakers* are available in almost every nation and are always willing to share their scientific and biblical knowledge.

Don't Forget Prayer and the Holy Spirit

It is not enough to simply destroy wrong philosophies, since destroying a man's philosophy may also destroy the man. Nor is it enough to replace evolutionary dogma with the Creation foundation. Even Creationists can fall short of eternal paradise unless they confess their sins and are reborn in Christ. Therefore, the prime aim of Creation evangelism is to preach the gospel, which begins in Genesis, as we have seen. Don't stop with just the scientific aspects of creation. It is vital to share Genesis and the entire gospel.

Remember, too, that facts alone will not win converts. It is the Holy Spirit who convinces through the Word of God. Pray that God will restrain Satan from people's lives and allow their eyes to be opened to truth. Teach new believers about the power of prayer. Thousands of Christians can testify that they came to Christ because someone took the time to do these things and share the necessary information.

Imagine what could happen if more and more churches started to stand up for Creation. This kind of evangelism could be the start of a great revival. For the first time, many Christians would begin to truly understand the Creation foundation of their faith. Their lives would become more stable and their witness more credible. What a wonderful difference this could make!

We especially recommend that all new Christians be channeled into a good Bible study on the Book of Genesis, so that they will come to a complete, foundational knowledge of what Christianity is all about. (*The Genesis Record* by Dr. Henry Morris is recommended as the single best and most accurate guide to Genesis.) Creation evangelism will elicit such enthusiastic responses as:

1. "My faith has been restored in the Scriptures."
2. "God seems so much more personal and ever-present now."
3. "For the first time, I really feel that I understand Christianity."
4. "God's Word is Truth."
5. "True science supports exactly what the Scriptures say."

Unlike atheism, Christianity is not a "blind" faith. It is actually quite objective, and God requires us to be able to give reasons for what we believe. As Peter said: ". . . Always be prepared to give an answer to everyone who asks you to give the reason for the hope that you have. But do this with gentleness and respect. . ." (1 Peter 3:15–16).

Give Creationist Ministries
Your Encouragement

We believe that Creationist ministries are among the most important ministries of our day. God has raised them up worldwide to provide Christians with the necessary tools for evangelizing our society. But if God's people do not take up these tools, the church will suffer for having neglected to effectively proclaim God's truth to the world.

Creation evangelism is one of the most important means of spreading the gospel today. Take up the challenge! Help restore the Genesis foundation to Christianity. There is a war on. Are you involved in the battle and its foundational issues? Every Christian must be a soldier for the Creator.

Subject Index

Aborigines, 82–83, 94
Abortion, 10, 46, 47, 51, 90, 91–92, 93, 97, 101, 102
Absolutes, 44, 45, 46
Adam and Eve, creation of, 69, 76–77
Adultery, 90
Agnostics, bias of, 14–15
Atheism, 91
Atheists, bias of, 13–14

Babel, *See* Tower of
Bias, choosing your, 17–22; evolution and, 18; of agnostics, 14–15; of atheists, 13–14; of Bible-believing Christians, 15
"Big Bang," 59

Carnivorous, 35, 36, 57, 60, 116
Chalmers, Thomas, 60
Christian ethics, 45
Christian schools, 106–07
Christian worldview, 89–90
"Chronologic teaching," 115
Clothing, and Genesis connection, 84–88
Communism, 96–97, 108
Creation, complete, 29, 83; evangelism, 109–119; literal six days, 9, 55, 58, 68

Creation/Evolution battle, 10
Creation Science, 56, 63
Creation Week, 60, 62; six day, 9, 55, 58, 61, 68
Creationism, 18, 103; biblical, 18; Progressive, 60, 67; scientific, 18, 22
Creator, born as a man, 31
Custance, Arthur C., 61

Darwin, Charles, 60, 93, 96, 97
Day-Age theory, 58; problems with, 56–57
Death, 37–42
Divorce, easy, 46, 47, 73–74
Drugs, 101

Earth, age of, 66–67
Ethics, Christian, 45; situation, 47
Euthanasia, 97
Evangelism, and creation, 109–19
Evening and morning, 58
Evolution, 18, 20; and abortion, 91; and communism, 96–97; and racism, 93–94; and the Gospel, 65; and moral absolutes, 90–99; God's use of, 55–63; 65–71; results of belief in, 97–99; theory of, 19, 23, 65
Evolutionary process, 56

121

Scripture Index

Genesis

1—29, 58
1–2—56
1–11—101
1:1—29, 60, 61, 63
1:2—60, 61, 62, 63
1:3—58
1:16—47
1:26–28—29
1:27—29, 74, 77
1:28—75
1:28a—29
1:29—36
1:29–30—36, 58
1:31—29, 58, 67
2:1–2—29
2:2—26
2:2–3—58
2:7—25, 29
2:7–8—77
2:9—60
2:15—60
2:16–17—25, 29
2:18—30
2:18–23—77
2:19—29
2:19–20—60
2:21–23—77
2:22–23—30

2:22–24—77
2:23—60, 74
2:24—30, 73
2:25—86
3—69
3:1–6—26
3:5—29
3:7—86
3:8—29
3:10—86
3:11—29
3:13—77
3:14–19—30
3:15—26
3:16—30, 77
3:17—30
3:18–20—30
3:19—26, 30
3:20—29, 77
3:21—86
3:22–23—30, 35
3:24—30
4:1–15—69
4:2b—60
4:10—29
4:11–12—30
4:17b—60
4:20–22—60
5:1—29
5:2—29, 74

6–9—69
6:5—29
6:5–7—30
6:11–12—70
6:13b—70
6:19–20—70
7:2–4—70
7:4—70
7:11–12—70
7:19–20—70
7:24—70
7:21–23—70
8:3–5—70
8:13–14—70
8:21—70
9:1—70, 75
9:3—36
9:13–15
9:11—70
9:15—70
11—30
11:1–9—69
12:1—30
18–19—69
18–25—25
19—75
19:4–6—30
19:13—30
26:5—29
35:11—75